Euripides

Cyclops

AN INTERMEDIATE
ANCIENT GREEK READER

C. T. Hadavas

Euripides: *Cyclops*

An Intermediate Ancient Greek Reader
Ancient Greek text with vocabulary and commentary

First Edition

© 2017 C. T. Hadavas

All rights reserved. This book may not be reproduced, in whole or in part, in any form (beyond copying permitted by Sections 107 and 108 of the U.S. Copyright Law and except by reviewers for the public press), without written permission from the publisher.

ISBN-13: 978-1979705516
ISBN-10: 1979705518

Published by C. T. Hadavas

Cover Design: C. T. Hadavas

Cover Image: The cover image (© Fondazione Sorgente Group, Rome), a mask of Papposilenus, is used by permission of, and with full credits to, Fondazione Sorgente Group, Rome.

Fonts: (English) Times New Roman, Book Antiqua; (Greek) GFS Porson

hadavasc@beloit.edu

TABLE OF CONTENTS

Preface	v
How to Use this Book	vii
Bibliographic Abbreviations	viii
Rhetorical/Literary Figures and Grammatical Terms	ix
Abbreviations	xii
Cover Image – Mask of Papposilenus	xiv
Euripides, *Cyclops*	1
Euripides	2
Satyrs	3
Satyr Play	4
Sophists	7
Euripides and Homer	10
A Play of Incongruities	11
Text	12
Bibliography	12
Translations	13
Meter	13
Cyclops	16
Other Ancient Greek and Latin Intermediate Readers by the Author	135

Preface

The story of Odysseus' encounter with the Cyclops Polyphemus (*Odyssey* 9.105-566) is probably the most famous of his adventures in Homer's *Odyssey* (c. 700 BCE). In fact, Homer's tale of the one-eyed giant proved so popular that it was retold (often in radically new ways) in many different visual, dramatic, and literary works throughout antiquity.[1] This edition of Euripides' *Cyclops* (possibly 408 BCE[2]), the earliest extant post-Homeric work of Ancient Greek "Cyclopea", is a companion piece to *Ancient Greek Cyclops Tales*, a text that contains, in addition to *Odyssey* 9.105-566, all of the other extant cyclopic works written in Ancient Greek (Theocritus' *Idylls* 6 and 11; Callimachus' Epigram 46 Pf./G-P 3; Lucian's *Dialogues of the Sea-Gods* 1 and 2).

In addition to providing students with brief introductory sections that touch on various aspects of Euripides and his unusual play, this edition offers extensive grammatical and lexical assistance, with notes focusing on the drama's cultural context as well as the thematic and intertextual connections with its source, *Odyssey* 9.105-566.

Together with *Ancient Greek Cyclops Tales*, these two editions offer students access to a collection of works—each fascinating in its own right—that span nearly nine centuries and are united by a single theme, thus facilitating a variety of diachronic comparative analyses.

---

[1] For the Cyclops depicted in ancient art, see the *Lexicon Iconographicum Mythologiae Classicae* (1981-2009) s.vv. "Kyklops" and "Polyphemos." There were at least three comedies and one satyr play—all nearly entirely lost—featuring Homer's Cyclops: Epicharmus' *Cyclops* (c. 500-450 BCE); Cratinus' *Odysseuses* (c. 455-420 BCE); Antiphanes' *Cyclops* (c. 380-340 BCE); Aristias' satyr play *Cyclops* (c. 470-460). In Latin literature, two essential cyclopic texts are Vergil, *Aeneid* 3.568-691 and Ovid, *Metamorphoses* 13.738-897. In addition to "Cyclops-centered" works, literary allusions to Homer's Cyclops tale also occur in Ancient Greek literature (e.g., in Aristophanes' comedy *Wasps* [422 BCE], which references in lines 179-187 both Odysseus' escape from the Cyclops' cave by clinging to the bottom of a ram and his (in)famous naming of himself to the Cyclops as "No-man").

[2] R. Seaford, *The Journal of Hellenic Studies*, Vol. 102 (1982), pp. 161-172.

How To Use This Book

The reader is assumed to have a basic acquaintance with Ancient Greek grammar. All vocabulary found in the passage of each text on the left page, with the exception of the verb εἰμί, personal pronouns, and the most common conjunctions (e.g., ἀλλά, καί), adverbs (e.g., οὐ, μή), and particles (e.g., μέν, δέ), is given on the facing page. For many verbs only the first person singular present active indicative form is provided. For verbs with unusual forms (e.g., those with deponent futures, second aorists, or with futures and aorists from unrelated stems) the first person singular active forms of the present, future, and aorist are, where warranted, given. For -μι verbs the second aorist active and/or the perfect active, where warranted, are also provided.

On the understanding that the majority of readers who will use this text have either just finished the first or second year of college Ancient Greek, or are returning after a hiatus of some time from their study of the language, I have provided extensive grammatical notes. Although such notes are not exhaustive, they do identify—and sometimes explicate—certain aspects of Ancient Greek (e.g., idioms, non-indicative verb usages, genitive absolutes, etc.) about which many students in their second and third year of study still have questions. In addition to such linguistic assistance, the notes also identify literary/rhetorical tropes and select grammatical terms, make reference to intertextual connections with other cyclopic works and themes, and provide brief explanations of people, places, and things that will probably be unfamiliar to many readers.

Bibliographic Abbreviations

Kovacs	Kovacs, D. *Euripides. Cyclops. Alcestis. Medea.* Cambridge (MA), 1994
Long	Long, W. E. *Euripides. Cyclops.* Oxford, 1891
Olson	Olson, S. D. *Euripides' Cyclops.* (Bryn Mawr Commentaries). Bryn Mawr (PA), 1999
O'Sullivan and Collard	O'Sullivan, P. and C. Collard. *Euripides. Cyclops and Major Fragments of Greek Satyric Drama.* Oxford, 2013
Seaford	Seaford, R. *Euripides. Cyclops.* Clarendon Press: Oxford, 1984
Tosheva-Nikolovska	Tosheva-Nikolovska, D. "Satyr-Play: Tragedy at Play or Mockery Drama?" in *Živa Antika*, Monographs No. 10: Ad perpetuam memoriam Michaelis D. Petruševski, Skopje, 2012, pp. 271-93
Ussher	Ussher, R. G. "The 'Cyclops' of Euripides. *Greece & Rome* Vol. 18, No. 2 (Oct. 1971), pp. 166-179
Waterfield	Waterfield, R. *Euripides: Heracles and Other Plays.* Oxford, 2008

Rhetorical/Literary Figures and Grammatical Terms

alliteration (*alliteratio*, Latin *ad* [expressing addition] + *littera*, "letter") occurs when a sound of the first letter in a series of multiple words is repeated.

anacoluthon (ἀνακόλουθον, "not following *or* agreeing"), or grammatical inconsistency, is inadvertent or purposed deviation in the structure of a sentence by which a construction started at the beginning is not followed out consistently. Anacoluthon is sometimes real, sometimes only slight and apparent. It is natural to Greek by reason of the mobility and elasticity of that language; but in English it is not tolerated to an equal extent because that language—a speech of few inflected forms—is much more rigid than Greek.

anastrophe (ἀναστροφή, "turning back," "return") occurs in the case of oxytone prepositions of two syllables, which throw the accent back on the first syllable. This occurs most often in verse when the preposition follows its case: τούτων πέρι (for περὶ τούτων) "about these things."

apposition (*adpositio*, Latin "placement near") is a grammatical construction in which two elements, normally noun phrases, are placed side by side, with one element serving to identify the other in a different way. The two elements are said to be "in apposition."

assonance (*assonare*, Latin "respond to" [< *ad*, "to" + *sonare*, "to sound"]) occurs when when two or more words close to one another repeat the same vowel sound but start with different consonant sounds.

asyndeton (ἀσύνδετον, "not bound together") occurs when two or more sentences (or words) independent in form and thought, are juxtaposed, i.e. coordinated without any connective. The absence of connectives in a language so rich in means of coordination as is Greek is more striking than in other languages. Rhetorical asyndeton generally expresses emotion of some sort, and is the mark of liveliness, rapidity, passion, or impressiveness of thought, each idea being set forth separately and distinctly.

chiasmus (χιασμός, "marking with diagonal lines" [like an "X"]) is the crosswise arrangement of contrasted pairs to give alternate stress. By this figure both the extremes and the means are correlated.

figura etymologica (*figura*, Latin "[rhetorical] figure" + *etymologica*, Latin [< Gk. ἐτυμολογική, "belonging to etymology"]) occurs when words with the same etymological derivation are used adjacently. To count as a *figura etymologica*, it is necessary that the two words be genuinely different words and not just different inflections of the same word. In Homer, it occurs when a verb governs its related noun.

hendiadys (ἓν διὰ δυοῖν, "one through two") is the use of two words connected by a copulative conjunction to express a single complex idea; especially two substantives instead of one substantive and an adjective or attributive genitive.

hypallage (ὑπαλλαγή, "exchange") is a change in the relation of words by which a word, instead of agreeing with the case it logically qualifies, is made to agree grammatically with another case.

hyperbaton (ὑπέρβατον, "transposition") is the separation of words naturally belonging together. Such displacement usually gives prominence to the first of two words thus separated, but sometimes to the second also. In prose, hyperbaton is less common than in poetry, but even in prose it is frequent, especially when it secures emphasis on an important idea by placing it at the beginning or end of a sentence. At times hyperbaton may mark passionate excitement. Sometimes it was adopted to gain rhythmical effect.

hysteron proteron (ὕστερον πρότερον, "latter before") occurs when the first key word or phrase of the idea refers to something that happens temporally later than the second key word or phrase. The goal of *hysteron proteron* is to call attention to the more important idea by placing it first.

litotes (λιτότης, "plainness", "simplicity") is (often ironic) understatement so as to intensify. Something is stated by denying its opposite, particularly the negation of a negative quality to say something positive.

metonomy (μετωνυμία, "change of name") is the substitution of one word for another to which it stands in some close relation.

paronomasia (παρονομασία, "word play") is a play upon words which sound alike.

pluralis maiestatis (Latin, "[the] plural of majesty"; aka, "the royal 'we' ") is the use of plural pronouns and/or corresponding plural-inflected verb forms to refer to a single person. Most often occuring in verse, *pluralis maiestatis* frequently is used to grant dignity to the singular. In comic works, however, there is often an incongruous connection between the person employing *pluralis maiestatis* and the notion of dignity.

tautology (ταὐτολογία, "sameness of expression") occurs when a word or statement unnecessarily repeats the meaning of another word. Although its use in everyday speech is generally indicative of carelessness or clumsiness, in literary texts it can also signal emphasis or nervousness.

tmesis (τμῆσις, "cutting") is a linguistic phenomenon in which a verb is separated into two parts (its prepositional prefix and the verb itself), with other words interrupting between them. In Homer, the literal meaning of *tmesis* is a misnomer, since the prefix had not yet evolved linguistically into becoming part of the verb.

ABBREVIATIONS

= is equivalent to
< derived from
< > material within these marks has been inserted to complete sense and/or meter in the readings contained in the manuscripts of the play
[ ] (in vocabulary) hypothetical reconstruction of non-extant form; (in notes) understood words supplied by this author; (in Greek text) material within these marks appears to be a later addition to the text and not a part of Euripides' original play
acc.(usative)
act.(ive voice)
adj.(ective)
adv.(erb)
aor.(ist)
c. circa
C-to-F = Contrary to Fact
cf. (*confer*, Latin "bring together") compare
ch.(apter)
cl.(ause)
comp.(arative)
condit.(ion)
conj.(unction)
contr.(acted)
dat.(ive)
dep.(opent)
dim.(inutive)
dir.(ect)
esp.(ecially)
exclam.(ation)
fem.(inine)
FLV = future less vivid (aka, future remote)
FMV = future move vivid
freq.(uently)
fut.(ure)
gen.(itive)
gen.(itive) abs.(olute)
Gk. = Greek
impera.(tive)

imperf.(ect)
indecl.(inable)
indic.(ative)
indir.(ect)
inf.(initive)
masc.(uline)
mid.(dle voice)
neut.(er)
n.(ote)
nom.(inative)
Od.(yssey)
obj.(ect)
opt.(ative)
p./pp. page(s)
part.(iciple)
pass.(ive voice)
perf.(ect)
pl.(ural)
pluperf.(ect)
pres.(ent)
prob.(ably)
pron.(oun)
rel.(ative) cl.(ause)
rel.(ative) pron.(oun)
(S) appears occasionally in Olson's notes where it refers to Seaford's commentary (see **BIBLIOGRAPHIC ABBREVIATIONS** above) whenever his "debts to [Seaford] are most substantial"
s.v. (*sub verbo*, Latin, "under the word"); s.vv. (*sub verbis*, Latin, "under the words") [used to refer to an entry/entries in a dictionary or encyclopedia]
sc. (*scilicet* < *scire licet*, Latin "it is permitted to know") = supply *or* understand
sing.(ular)
subj.(ect)
subju.(nctive)
superl.(ative)
usu.(ally)
vb. = verb
vb. adj. = verbal adjective
voc.(ative)

Cover Image – Mask of Papposilenus

The image employed on the cover of this commentary, "Mask of Papposilenus," is accompanied on the Fondazione Sorgente Group website by the following text (http://www.fondazionesorgentegroup.com/Mask-of-Papposilenus__archaeology_list_21.html):

"The bronze mask is a unicum in Greek-Roman artistic production. According to the research of Prof. Eugenio La Rocca it depicts Papposilenus: a semi-wild being with a round face dominated by a thick dishevelled beard and a completely bald head. His animal nature is revealed in the shape of his ears (equine) and, in versions including the entire figure, his tail, hairy fur that completely covers his arms and legs and, at times, horse's hooves.

Found at sea, as is evident in the surface concretions not entirely eliminated during previous cleanings, it was brought to Italy when acquired by the Sorgente Group and was displayed and presented to the public for the first time at the museum headquarters of the National Museum of Rome in Palazzo Altemps (16 April/18 July 2010).

The subject depicted is the oldest silenus (the meaning of his name).... One of the masks used in satyr plays was that of Papposilenus, which, over time, acquired the same general appearance of the masks of the commedia with increasingly grotesque forms. The mask, of extremely fine workmanship and exceptional size, is one of the rarest examples in bronze dating from the Hellenistic age, perhaps around the first half of the 1st century BC. It is completely hollow on the backside, making it extremely light. Two quadrangular holes on the edges of the ears probably served to hang the mask with a looped ribbon: it is thus likely that it was originally displayed in a peristyle with a garden in a rich residence, the mask fluttering between the columns, hung by plant garlands to complement the numerous other decorative elements in the environment: decorated disks (called oscilla since they were hung, like the bronze mask, between the columns), figurative reliefs leaning on small pillars, small and large marble statues in the round and fountains..."

Euripides

Cyclops

EURIPIDES

The Athenian tragedian Euripides (*c*. 480-*c*. 406 BCE) wrote 92-95 plays, of which 18-19 survive.[3] Most famous for his *Medea*, *Hippolytus*, *Trojan Women*, and *Bacchae*, Euripides was the youngest of the three great tragic playwrights—Aeschylus (*c*. 535-*c*. 455 BCE) and Sophocles (497/6-406/5 BCE) were the other two—active in Athens in the fifth century.

Although popular in his day (both specific verses and sometimes whole scenes, for example, were constantly being appropriated by comic playwrights, especially Aristophanes [*c*. 446-*c*. 386 BCE], for parodic purposes), Euripides rarely was accorded first prize by the judges.[4] Nevertheless, he seems to capture, perhaps better than any other writer of his time, the shifting intellectual and cultural currents of the last three decades or so of the fifth century. His posthumous popularity, however, became so great that when revivals of fifth-century plays (now considered "classics") began to be staged in later centuries, his works quickly became staples of the performance repertoire. Indeed, the number of these post fifth-century performances of Euripides' plays completely eclipsed those of Aeschylus and Sophocles. In addition, he appears to have been studied widely throughout the Late Antique period (beginning *c*. 200 CE), with ten of his plays virtually becoming school texts.

---

[3] Scholars differ on whether or not to include *Rhesus*, a drama which stylistically does not seem very Euripidean and is in all probability a 4th-century BCE work.

[4] In fact, he only was awarded first prize on five occasions (four of which were while he was alive). Aeschylus and Sophocles, by contrast, were far more successful in this regard, winning first prize 13 and 18 times, respectively. Of course, simply being selected as one of the three playwrights each year whose plays were given the honor of performances at the City Dionysia (the only time tragedies were performed in Athens during the fifth century) was already a "win" in one respect. Since Euripides wrote around 92 plays, that means he would have been chosen on 23 different occasions to have one of his tetralogies (three different tragedies plus a satyr play) performed before the Athenian *demos*. Given the fact that Euripides first competed in the City Dionysia in 455 BCE, it seems that for approximately half of the total years of his active career Euripides was selected by the authorities to have his plays performed.

In addition to their continuing public popularity, Euripides' dramatic works, with their innovations in "genre-mixing" (i.e., his combination of tragic, comic, romantic, melodramatic, and political elements, often within a single play) had a profound effect on both the development of New Comedy (*c.* 323-c. 260 BCE) and Roman drama, especially the tragedies of Seneca (*c.* 4 BCE-65 CE). In fact, it was through Seneca that Euripides would influence still later generations of playwrights, including the Elizabethans (most famously Shakespeare [1564-1616]). By the middle of the seventeenth century, Euripides, both in translation and in the original Greek, had become widely read again in France, and it was at this time that he, together with Seneca, had a deep and lasting impact on the greatest of all French tragedians, Jean Racine (1639-1699).

SATYRS

Bizarre hybridizations of man, animal (at first bits of horses, later also parts of goats), and the divine, satyrs are, first and foremost, devoted servants of Dionysus (god of wine and theater who is capable of transforming his worshipers' mental states) and members of his *thiasos*—the religiously-inflected ecstatic retinue of inebriated revelers who accompany the god. The often perplexing, and at times even paradoxical, social and psychological nature of satyrs can present challenges in comprehending these peculiar mythological creatures. Here are two contemporary scholars' views of satyrs:

1. Edith Hall (in Waterfield, xxx) enumerates "the magic of these complex and charming creatures" by noting how, "like their master Dionysus, satyrs confound many of the polarities by which the Greeks organized their perception of the world. They are nearly human, yet are touched with the divine and have tails, animal ears, and often hoofs. They are cowardly yet violent. They are often bald and yet always childlike. They are sly and knowing, but simultaneously naive and innocent. They are often involved in the gods' inventions of the arts of civilization..., but live in remote, uncultivated countryside.... The one boundary satyrs do not cross is that demarcating male from female. They are exaggeratedly male from the biological point of view (erections are a recurrent feature of satyr drama), and decidedly homosocial—they live with members of

their own sex, and spend their time on collective male pursuits: hunting, athletics, drinking, and chasing nymphs. In the female-free environment of *Cyclops* the satyrs can only fantasize about rape, but in many other satyr plays the plot revolved around sexual aggression against females."

2. Rush Rehm (588), on the other hand, in his review of Mark Griffith's important collection of five essays on satyr plays, notes that, "In his [i.e., Griffith's] view, many males [in the audience] would have identified with these half-man, half-goat *daimones*, 'puerile-servile' creatures who remain 'accountable to nobody for their behavior' (p. 44) and yet offered the audience a compelling 'choral perspective.' (p. 15). Their collaboration with mythic heroes in a romantic plot delivers a restorative outcome that rescues satyr drama from the sober, morally inflected, *polis*-riddled and 'aristocratizing' (pp. 34, 95) tendencies of tragedy... G[riffith]. acknowledges the speculative nature of these suggestions. So he might excuse some of us for wondering if fifth-century Athenians had any such notion of identity-formation via adoptive subject-positions, and if so, how many would have identified with a group of morally and mentally infantilised adults, slaves to the desire for drink and sex, cowards in the extreme, with permanently erect penises (tiresome, painful?)."[5]

While reading Euripides' *Cyclops*, the student should observe how the playwright both employs the satyrs structurally and thematically in his drama, and how he characterizes them and their father Silenus, especially with regard to the views of these creatures as described by the two scholars above.

SATYR PLAY

In fifth-century BCE Athens, Greek dramatic performances were in many ways quite different from those of later periods. Plays were performed outdoors in an open-air theater as part of a religious festival in honor of the god Dionysus known as the City Dionysia.

---

[5] R. Rehm, *Classical Review* 66.2 (2016), p. 588 (review of Griffith, M. *Greek Satyr Play. Five Studies.* (California Classical Studies 3). Berkeley, 2015).

This five-day festival, which took place in late March-early April, was the only time tragedies were performed during the year. After a number of playwrights had submitted their plays for consideration, only three were selected to have their dramas entered into competition. Each of the tragic playwrights then had four of his dramatic works performed on the same day (comic playwrights only composed a single work for competition). After three days of competition, first, second, and third prizes were awarded. The four works that a tragic dramatist created consisted of three tragedies and one satyr play. With regard to the latter, however, there seems to have been some flexibility in terms of offering an occasional substitution (e.g., Euripides' *Alcestis* [438 BCE] took the fourth slot traditionally reserved for a satyr play; and although this play contains traces of thematic and structural elements common to satyric drama—Heracles' drunkenness and his defeat of a "monster" [i.e., Death]—, it is most emphatically not a satyr play).

In the West, ancient tragedies have, with the exception of an (admittedly) lengthy hiatus during the Middle Ages, never completely ceased to be performed. Even during the Middle Ages, Byzantine scholars continued to copy and study a select group of twenty-four plays by Aeschylus, Sophocles, and Euripides.[6] Today, despite such unusual elements rarely seen in later works of this dramatic genre (e.g., its use of masks, the prominence of a large chorus consisting of 12-15 actors, the incorporation of song and dance sequences), ancient tragedy is still readily understood and appreciated by contemporary audiences and readers. Indeed, revivals and adaptations of these dramas are performed with some regularity on stages throughout the world.

The satyr play, however, unlike tragedy, is a theatrical genre unknown to nearly everyone today who is not a classicist. There are

---

[6] The *Cyclops* [Κύκλωψ] was not one of Euripides' plays that made it into the school curriculum. Instead, it is one of his nine so-called "alphabetic plays," a selection from his collected works that was arranged alphabetically (all of the plays' titles that survive from this group—preserved in a single late medieval manuscript—begin with the Greek letters H, I, and K). These nine plays are valuable in terms of understanding Euripides' wide-ranging experiments in playwrighting since they preserve a random selection of his works and not simply those deemed important by ancient scholars and teachers.

two reasons why this is so: (1) its lifespan only lasted around 250-300 years. After a quick ascent at the end of the sixth century BCE, the satyr play apparently reached its peak in terms of aesthetic innovation (and possibly popularity) in the first half of the fifth century BCE. Around 340 BCE the satyr play no longer occupied the fourth slot in a tragic playwright's tetralogy, but had an independent existence.[7] The genre seems to have finally died out sometime in the third century BCE; (2) only one satyr play, Euripides' *Cyclops*, is completely extant.

Aristotle believed that tragedy developed out of the satyr play (*Poetics* 1449a), and whether his belief is correct or not, satyr plays, for all of their comic aspects, do partake of certain elements of ancient tragedy. In fact, satyr plays might perhaps be best understood, in the words of one ancient critic, as "tragedy at play" (Demetrius, *On Style* 169). Like ancient comedy, satyr plays are designed (at least in part) to make one laugh. Also like ancient comedy, satyr plays include bits of "indecency" (especially in terms of the—often ribald—verbal and physical antics of the phallus-wearing Satyrs and their father Silenus).[8] But like tragedy, a satyr play's plot is based on myth (although the plots of a few ancient comedies are also based on myth—see p. v fn. 1 above for three examples—, most are fictional tales grounded in the contemporary world).[9] Indeed, satyr plays, by ridiculing aspects of the particular myths which form their respective plots, seem to be asking their audiences to reconsider such stories and the characters that inhabit them from a somewhat different, slightly off-kilter perspective. But not *too* different, at least plot-wise, for in the end, although the satyrs "crash" the myth that makes up the plot of the play, the original

---

[7] Tosheva-Nikolovska, 281.

[8] Cf., e.g., *Cyclops* 169-172.

[9] This is not to say that *all* fifth-century BCE tragedies had plots taken from myth. In addition to a few based on history (e.g., Aeschylus' *Persians* [472 BCE], which recounts the Persian reaction to the defeat of their forces by the Greeks at the Battle of Salamis eight years earlier, a battle that had quickly evolved in the Athenian consciousness to the point of becoming "mythologized"), we know of only one instance, Agathon's (no longer extant) *Anthos*, which had a truly invented plot (Aristotle, *Poetics* 1456a). These plays, however, are the very rare exceptions that prove the rule.

outcome of the mythical story holds. Lastly, the language of a satyr play, particularly that spoken in the *Cyclops* by the original characters of that myth (Odysseus and Polyphemus), leans ever so slightly more towards the stylized, "elevated" discourse of tragedy than towards the more colloquial speech of comedy (though there is much of that as well, especially in terms of the language used by Silenus and the chorus of satyrs).[10]

SOPHISTS

Between *c.* 450-*c.* 375 BCE an intellectual revolution occurred in the Greek world that had a profound influence on society and its cultural, political, and philosophical movers and shakers. This movement came about through the activities of itinerant professional educators, known as sophists, who taught a variety of courses for (often extraordinary amounts of) money. Their students primarily consisted of young Athenian artistocratic elites who had come to believe that they needed to gain some sort of additional advantage— especially in politics and in the courts (in which, in addition to legal issues, much political power now resided)—over their fellow citizens of lesser economic status. The reasons for this are complex, but can probably be traced primarily to two interdependent developments that had a transformative impact on fifth-century Athenian society: (1) political reforms initiated by Pericles (*c.* 495-429 BCE) and Ephialtes (assassinated in 461 BCE) in 462 BCE that led (nominally, at first, but in many cases effectively as the century developed) to all male Athenian citizens possessing (more or less) equal political power (i.e., the so-called "radical" democracy); (2) the expanding economic, political, military, and cultural power of Athens and its imperial democracy at this time, which provided a greater influx of monetary resources into Athens from its tribute-paying "allies," thus allowing the Athenian *polis* to pay many of its citizens to participate in a wide variety of public affairs.

---

[10] For a brief overview of satyr plays' linguistic relationship to tragedy and comedy, see Tosheva-Nikolovska, 276-8; for a more detailed analysis, see A. L. Eire, "La lengua del drama satírico," *Minerva* 15 (2001), pp. 137-160.

Although sophists taught a variety of subjects (including music, astronomy, mathematics, and linguistics), many specialized in teaching others how to deploy the tools of philosophy and rhetoric to better achieve one's goals in life by convincing others of the validity of one's own point of view. Since the ultimate objective was winning the argument (and thus be in a better position to satisfy one's desires, even at the expense of others' well-being), sophists and their students came to be regarded with great suspicion both by non-elite citizens and by moral philosophers such as Plato (*c.* 425-348/7 BCE). After all, the very first sophist, Protagoras of Abdera (*c.* 490-*c.* 420 BCE), had declared that "man is the measure of all things." This idea, his critics claimed, had provided the (intellectually suspect, in their eyes) basis for the grounding of one's moral outlook on life in terms of relativism: there is no absolute truth, only one's own "truths" that may or may not be in agreement with another person's "truths."

The fictional character who appears most transformed by this sophistic revolution is that of Odysseus. In the majority of tragedies in which this hero has a significant presence (Sophocles' *Philoctetes*, Euripides' *Hecuba* and [the no longer extant] *Palamedes*), Odysseus' character is depicted as a consummate sophist-politician who places expedience above ethics. The ironic twist with Euripides' *Cyclops* is that it flips this script, since it portrays Odysseus as largely an adherent of heroic Homeric beliefs and of traditional fifth-century mores even as his (formerly primitive) enemy, the Cyclops, is depicted as embracing the new sophistic ideologies with their concomitant focus on satisfying one's (mostly physical) desires.

Indeed, in Euripides' play, Polyphemus is clearly the more radically altered character of the two principals from Homer's tale. Freed from the shackles placed on him by the Odyssean first-person narrative perspective of *Odyssey* 9, this one-time giant ogre has been transformed into a (caricature of a) late fifth-century BCE Athenian aristocratic elite: he now is both a cattle- and sheep-rancher who uses slaves (the satyrs) to run his herding operations, goes hunting (an aristocratic pursuit), and overall appears to be an individual of some wealth. In addition, he has developed a more refined palate. If not quite a gourmet, his culinary expertise is far more developed than that of his Homeric alter-ego, who satisfied his taste for human flesh prepared only one way: raw. When it comes to liquid refreshment, this late fifth-century Polyphemus no longer enjoys only sheep's milk, but now has multiple dairy options available to slake his thirst, including a "mixed" drink consisting of both cow's and sheep's milk—a joke meant to portray the Cyclops as ludicrously attempting to imitate contemporary Greek oenophilic proclivities. This (somewhat incomplete) transformation from primitive monster to elite aristocrat is not entirely satirical, however, for although the Euripidean Cyclops never receives the opportunity to elicit the same amount of pity from the audience as his Homeric counterpart,[11] "he displays," as Ussher (174) notes, "more human qualities than Homer's: an instinctive generosity of spirit makes him anxious to share his good fortune with his brothers (445, 509, 531, 533) and he even has a rough-hewed sense of humor."

But perhaps the most distinctive aspect of the Euripidean Cyclops' characterization vis-à-vis his Homeric counterpart is his intellectual and ideological transformation: this Polyphemus, like many of the Athenian artistocratic elite in the audience, has apparently received an education at the hands of sophists. Whereas the Euripidean Odysseus seems to articulate a society based on the rule of law, Polyphemus' actions and ideas partake of anti-democratic / pro-tyrannical ideologies (most famously expressed in Plato's anti-sophistic dialogue *Gorgias* by the character Callicles), viz. that might makes right, that greed is good, and that wealth has now replaced religion. As Kovacs (55-56) well puts it: "[this Cyclops has] "seen through" traditional morality, and he regards law as an invention of man that needlessly complicates life.... [he is also] a sophisticated arguer who can articulately *justify* his immoral behavior. When Homer's Polyphemus neither knows nor cares about the Trojan War, in Euripides he has heard all about it and has an opinion about it. He clearly inhabits the same moral world as the Greeks but has chosen to reject a morality he knows perfectly well."

---

[11] This occurs when the Homeric Cyclops, after having been blinded by Odysseus and his men, addresses his beloved ram at *Od.* 447-460. This remarkable scene, full of pathos and dramatic tension (Odysseus is clinging to the underbelly of the ram during the speech), is one of the most moving (and sentimental) in the entire epic.

EURIPIDES AND HOMER

With the exception of the rather dramatic transformation made to the Cyclops' character, Euripides' appropriation of his source, *Odyssey* 9.105-566, appears at first glance somewhat more conservative. Indeed, one could argue that the playwright seems to simplify the rather complex themes and characterizations of his Homeric material mostly in order to follow conventional theatrical principles of the time. He does so by adding a chorus (a necessity in fifth-century drama) and employing standard theatrical practices (e.g., the main action of the play takes place outside, not inside, Polyphemus' cave, since in ancient drama all action takes place out-of-doors).

More innovative is Euripides' inclusion of a contemporary cultural practice that was unknown to Homer: a symposium, complete with excessive drinking, erotic banter and sexual activity. This newly created scene also contributes to the portrayal of the Cyclops as an aristocratic elite, since symposia were an essential component of such an individual's social life.

Although the startling transformation of the Cyclops' character and the anachronistic inclusion of a symposium strike readers as Euripides' most significant alteration and addition to Homer's tale, they are only the most obvious ways in which the playwright has fundamentally reoriented so many aspects of the original story. Upon closer inspection, for example, even Euripides' more conventional adaptations clearly reveal how often he goes beyond simple theatrical necessities in terms of revisiting the ethical questions generated by the actions of Homer's characters. Consider, for example, the shift of setting from inside the cave to outside. With the main action now taking place outside, the large boulder that functions in Homer's epic to seal the cave shut and prevent the Greeks from escaping is no longer required. This means that, in addition to there being no reason for the nighttime visit of the neighboring Cyclopes and the escape of Odysseus' men tied to the underbellies of the sheep, there is also *no longer a need* to blind the Cyclops to escape; in fact, the Greeks now only have to get him drunk in order to get away. The moral implications of this are fascinating, for the blinding now becomes solely an act of righteous retaliation for the Cyclops' outrageous and unjust actions of eating two of Odysseus' men.[12]

In fact, Euripides' transformation of Homer's story goes back to its very beginning, where the Athenian playwright has effected a radical change in motivation on the part of Odysseus for why he ended up in the Cyclops' cave in the first place. In contrast to the Homeric Odysseus' curiosity and (troubling) act of "trespassing/breaking and entering" (and, one might add, his helping himself to some of the Cyclops' readily available comestibles), the Euripidean Odysseus initiates with Silenus and the satyrs an open and honest attempt at bartering for much-needed food supplies, since it is not curiosity and a desire for guest-gifts that motivate him as they did in Homer, but simple necessity.

A PLAY OF INCONGRUITIES

The *Cyclops* raises numerous incongruities in terms of plot, themes, and characterization, especially in relation to its Homeric source and the nature of contemporary Athenian society as filtered through the peculiar sensibilities of its author. As Seaford (56) astutely notes in this regard: "Any serious thought that the play contains derives from the compatibility of Polyphemos' modern sophistication with his savagery, and much of the humour from their incompatibility. For example, the fastidiousness of his concern with his (barbarous) milk... and the Hellenic modernity of his cannibalism invest the old story with a sense of unreality... This sense is reinforced by the presence of the satyrs. We are faced in fact with a multiple incongruity, between the Homeric folk-tale, the loftiness of tragedy, the rhetorical expression of contemporary intellectual debate characteristic of Euripidean tragedy, and the Dionysiac world of the *thiasos*."

---

[12] Without the boulder, there is no longer any logical reason preventing the Greeks from killing the Cyclops in Euripides' play, something they cannot do in Homer's story or else they will remain trapped within his cave. What does prevent them from doing so is simply the requirement of the original story, which only necessitates one fundamental action: the *blinding* of the Cyclops (cf. *Cyclops* 447-9 for Odysseus' explicit rejection of the idea that he should murder the Cyclops).

TEXT

The text is my own, though to a great extent based on that of

Kovacs, D. *Euripides: Cyclops, Alcestis, Medea.* Cambridge (MA), 1994

with the following differences:

170 παρεσκευασμένου for παρεσκευασμένον
321 ὅτι for ὅ τι
326 εὖ τέγγων τε γαστέρ᾽ ὕπτιος for ἑστιῶ τι γαστέρ᾽ ὑπτίαν
327 ἐπεκπιών for εἶτ᾽ ἐκπιών
    πέπλον for πλέων
343 τόνδε for ἅλα
355 Ζεῦ, for Ζεύς
398 θ᾽ ἑνὶ for τινι
398-399 w/ missing line after 399 for 399-398 w/ no missing line
413 παῖ for τοῦ
501 μυρόχριστος λιπαρόν for μυρόχριστον λιπαρός
620 κἀγώ for κᾆτ᾽ ἐγώ
692 Ὀδυσσέα for †Ὀδυσσέα†

BIBLIOGRAPHY

For a full bibliography, see O'Sullivan and Collard (59-71).

For excellent, if at times rather technical, introductions, see Seaford (1-60) and O'Sullivan and Collard (1-57)

For a detailed study of the *Cyclops* in terms of its relationship to its genre, an analysis of its plot and themes, in what ways it differs from its source (*Odyssey* 9.105-566), how it reflects and comments upon contemporary religious, philosophical, and literary trends, and an exploration of the staging and visual experience, see (forthcoming) C. Shaw, *Euripides: Cyclops: A Satyr Play* (Companions to Greek and Roman Tragedy), New York, 2018.

TRANSLATIONS

Arrowsmith, W. *Euripides V (The Bacchae, Iphigenia in Aulis, The Cyclops, Rhesus)*. 3rd ed. Chicago, 2013

Kovacs, D. *Euripides. Cyclops. Alcestis. Medea.* Cambridge (MA), 1994

McHugh, H. *Euripides: Cyclops*. Oxford, 2001

O'Sullivan, P. and C. Collard. *Euripides. Cyclops and Major Fragments of Greek Satyric Drama*. Oxford, 2013

Waterfield, R. *Euripides: Heracles and Other Plays*. Oxford, 2008

METER

Like all Greek drama, the *Cyclops* consists of iambic trimeters for the dialogue and a variety of different meters employed in the choral passages and songs. Although the meters used in the latter are relatively simple as far as dramatic choral lyrics go (see Seaford, 46-7), they are still rather complex for intermediate Ancient Greek students, and for that reason will not be explicated in this edition. For full metrical analyses of these choral lines (41-81, 356-74, 483-518, 608-23, 656-62), Seaford's commentary should be consulted.

The principal meter of the *Cyclops* is iambic trimeter, the meter most commonly employed in Greek tragedy. An iambic *metron* ("foot" or "measure") consists of an anceps (x), i.e., a syllable that can be either long (–) or short (⌣), followed by a cretic (– ⌣ –). Three of these together form an iambic trimeter:

$$x - \smile - | x - \smile - | x - \smile -$$

In addition, cretics allow resolution (the replacing of a long with two shorts) to take place, especially in the first two of the three iambs. Substitution can also occur (the most common are to replace the anceps (x) with an anapest (⌣ ⌣ –) or—more rarely—a dactyl (– ⌣ ⌣).

Note that the final syllable of an iambic trimeter can be either short or long, but is always counted as long (this is called *brevis in longo*).

The first five lines of the *Cyclops* thus scan as follows:

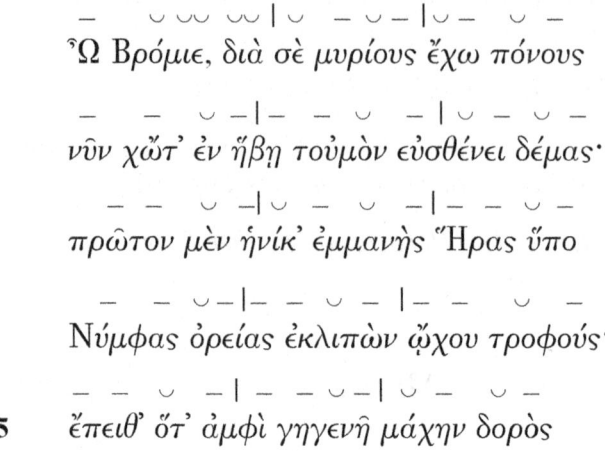

5 ἔπειθ᾽ ὅτ᾽ ἀμφὶ γηγενῆ μάχην δορὸς

Note that only the first of these five lines has a resolution (turning both long syllables of the first iambic metron's cretic [– ◡ –] into a series of five shorts [◡ ◡ ◡ ◡ ◡]).

ΚΥΚΛΩΨ

Σιληνός

Ὦ Βρόμιε, διὰ σὲ μυρίους ἔχω πόνους
νῦν χὤτ' ἐν ἥβῃ τοὐμὸν εὐσθένει δέμας·
πρῶτον μὲν ἡνίκ' ἐμμανὴς Ἥρας ὕπο
Νύμφας ὀρείας ἐκλιπὼν ᾤχου τροφούς·
5 ἔπειθ' ὅτ' ἀμφὶ γηγενῆ μάχην δορὸς
ἐνδέξιος σῷ ποδὶ παρασπιστὴς βεβὼς
Ἐγκέλαδον ἰτέαν ἐς μέσην θενὼν δορὶ
ἔκτεινα—φέρ' ἴδω, τοῦτ' ἰδὼν ὄναρ λέγω;

Σιληνός the old rustic god of wine-making and drunkenness. He was the foster-father of Dionysos, who was entrusted to his care by Hermes after his birth from the thigh of Zeus. The young god was raised by Silenus and nursed by the Nysiad nymphs in a cave on Mount Nysa

2 χὤτ' = καὶ ὅτε
τοὐμὸν = τὸ ἐμόν
εὐσθένει unaugmented vb.

3 Ἥρας Zeus' wife; she resented the illegitimate children whom the continually adulterous Zeus had w/ other women (in this case, the mortal Semele)
Ἥρας ὕπο when the prep. follows its noun/pron., the accent shifts to the first syllable (this is called *anastrophe*)

4 τροφούς in *apposition* to Νύμφας ὀρείας
ᾤχου 2nd sing. imperf. (= pluperf.) mid. (dep.) < οἴχομαι; often w/ part. (here ἐκλιπών); lit., 'you had gone off leaving behind,' i.e., you had gone off and left behind

5 γηγενῆ μάχην δορὸς lit., "the earthborn battle of the spear," i.e., the battle fought w/ spears against the Giants, the offspring of Ouranos ("Heaven") and Gaia ("Earth"). An example of *hypallage*

6 ἐνδέξιος σῷ ποδὶ lit. "on the right to your foot", i.e., "to your right." "Greek soldiers fought with their shield on their left arm, and a man was thus protected on his right

ἀμφί (prep. + acc.), during
βαίνω, walk, step; go; (perf.)
  take up one's position, stand
Βρόμιος, ὁ, (common name/
  epithet of Dionysus) Roarer
  (< βρόμιος, -α, -ον, noisy,
  boisterous)
γηγενής, -ές, born of Gaia (i.e.,
  Earth; an epithet of Titans and
  Giants)
δέμας, τό, body
διά (prep. + acc.), for the sake of,
  because of
δόρυ, δορός, τό, spear
Ἐγκέλαδος, ὁ Enceladus
ἐκλείπω, ἐξέλειπον, leave
  behind
ἐμμανής, -ές, maddened
ἐμός, -ή, -όν, my
ἐνδέξιος, -α, -ον, on the right
ἔπειτα (adv.), then
εὐσθενέω, be strong
ἥβη, ἡ, youth
ἡνίκα (adv.), when
Ἥρα, ἡ, Hera
θείνω, [ἔθενον] (aor.), strike
ἰτέα, ἡ, wicker shield
κτείνω, ἔκτεινα, kill, slay

λέγω, say, speak
μάχη, ἡ, battle
μέσος, -η, -ον, middle (of)
μυρίος, -α, -ον, numberless,
  countless, infinite
Νύμφη, ἡ, nymph
νῦν (adv.), now
οἴχομαι, go away or off (pres.
  usu. = perf., imperf. = pluperf.)
ὄναρ, τό, dream; (acc. sing. often
  as adv.) in a dream
ὁράω/ὁρῶ, εἶδον, see
ὄρειος, -α, -ον, of the
  mountains, mountain-haunting
ὅτε (adv.), when
οὗτος, αὕτη, τοῦτο, this; (pl.)
  these
παρασπιστής, -οῦ, ὁ,
  companion in arms
πόνος, ὁ, toil, labor; pain,
  suffering
πούς, ποδός, ὁ, foot
πρῶτον (adv.), first, in the first
  place
τροφός, ὁ/ἡ, one who nourishes
  and rears a child, nurse-maid
ὑπό (prep. + gen.), by

---

side primarily by his neighbor's shield rather than his own.
To serve another man's right was thus to be his guardian."
(Olson, 26)
βεβὼς masc. nom. sing. perf. act. part. < βαίνω

7 Ἐγκέλαδον a giant traditionally defeated by Athena
  δορὶ dat. of means

8 φέρ' pres. impera. of φέρω is nearly always used
  adverbially, i.e., "come now"; ἴδω 1st sing. aor. act. subju.
  < ὁράω/ὁρῶ; hortatory subju., i.e., "let me see!" φέρ' ἴδω is
  a comedic/colloquial phrase; Olson (26) suggests "now wait
  a minute!" and comments: "even Silenus finds this boast
  momentarily difficult to believe."

οὐ μὰ Δί', ἐπεὶ καὶ σκῦλ' ἔδειξα Βακχίῳ.
10 καὶ νῦν ἐκείνων μεῖζον' ἐξαντλῶ πόνον.
ἐπεὶ γὰρ Ἥρα σοι γένος Τυρσηνικὸν
ληστῶν ἐπῶρσεν, ὡς ὁδηθείης μακράν,
⟨ἐγὼ⟩ πυθόμενος σὺν τέκνοισι ναυστολῶ
σέθεν κατὰ ζήτησιν. ἐν πρύμνῃ δ' ἄκρᾳ
15 αὐτὸς βεβὼς ηὔθυνον ἀμφῆρες δόρυ,
παῖδες δ' ⟨ἐπ'⟩ ἐρετμοῖς ἥμενοι γλαυκὴν ἅλα
ῥοθίοισι λευκαίνοντες ἐζήτουν σ', ἄναξ.
ἤδη δὲ Μαλέας πλησίον πεπλευκότας
ἀπηλιώτης ἄνεμος ἐμπνεύσας δορὶ
20 ἐξέβαλεν ἡμᾶς τήνδ' ἐς Αἰτναίαν πέτραν,

---

10 ἐκείνων sc. πόνων; gen. of comparison, that here precedes its comp. adj. (which is not unusu. in Gk.)
11-12 In the *Homeric Hymn to Dionysus*, Dionysus is kidnapped by Etruscan pirates (though w/out Hera's involvement)
12 ὁδηθείης 2nd sing aor. pass. opt. < ὁδάω; opt. in a purp. cl. in secondary sequence
13 πυθόμενος sc. what had happened to you
    ναυστολῶ historical pres., which makes the narrative more vivid (English prefers imperf.)
14 σέθεν = σου
    ἐν πρύμνῃ δ' ἄκρᾳ "where the rudder was, but also where the least physical labor was required." (Olson, 27)
15 ἀμφῆρες δόρυ poetic circumlocution for "ship"
16-17 ⟨ἐπ'⟩ ἐρετμοῖς ἥμενοι...λευκαίνοντες the language takes on a Homeric coloring, perhaps in a parodic manner
    ἥμενοι masc. nom. pl. perf. (= pres.) mid. (dep.) part. < ἧμαι
    ῥοθίοισι dat. of means
18 Μαλέας a treacherous cape off the southeast Peloponnese where Odysseus is blown off-course (*Od.* 9.80-1) and launched into the fairy-tale world of his wanderings

Αἰτναῖος, -α, -ον, of or belonging to Aetna, Aetnean
ἄκρος, -α, -ον, farthest point or end (of), highest part (of)
ἅλς, ἁλός, ἡ, sea
ἀμφήρης, -ες, fitted on both sides; w/ oars on both sides
ἄναξ, ἄνακτος, ὁ, lord
ἄνεμος, ὁ, wind
ἀπηλιώτης, -ου, ὁ, (w/ or w/out ἄνεμος), (lit.) from the (rising) sun, i.e., from the east; east wind
αὐτός, -ή, -ό, (intensive adj.) -self; (pl.) -selves
Βάκχιος/Βάκχος, ὁ, Bacchus (common name/epithet of Dionysus)
γένος, -ους, τό, race
γλαυκός, -ή, -όν, bluish green or gray/grey
δείκνυμι, ἔδειξα (aor.), display
δόρυ, δορός, τό, beam of wood
ἐκβάλλω, throw overboard or ashore
ἐμπνέω, ἡ, blow upon (+ dat.)
ἐξαντλέω/ἐξαντλῶ, endure
ἐπεί (conj.), since, for; when
ἐπόρνυμι, ἐπῶρσα, rouse and stir up X (acc.) against Y (dat.)
ἐρετμόν, τό, oar
εὐθύνω, steer X (acc.) straight
Ζεύς, Διός, Διΐ, Δία, ὁ, Zeus
ζητέω, seek, search for
ζήτησις, -εως, ἡ, (often w/ κατά), seeking, searching for (+ gen.)

ἤδη (adv.), by this time, already
ἧμαι, sit
κατά (prep. + acc.), for the purpose of
λευκαίνω, make X (acc.) white, whiten X (acc.)
λῃστής, -οῦ, ὁ, pirate
μά (particle used in strong protestations and oaths), by (+ acc. of deity appealed to)
μακράν (fem. acc. sing. adj. used as adv.), far away
Μαλέα, ἡ, Malea
μείζων, -ον (gen. -ονος), greater
ναυστολέω/ναυστολῶ, sail, go by ship
ὀδάω, export and sell
ὅδε, ἥδε, τόδε, this; (pl.) these
παῖς, παιδός, ὁ, son, child
πέτρα, ἡ, rock (frequently of cliffs, ledges, etc. by the sea)
πλέω, sail
πλησίον (adv./prep. + gen.), near
πρύμνα, ἡ, stern
πυνθάνομαι, ἐπυθόμην, learn
ῥόθια, τά, splashings
σκῦλον, τό, (mostly in pl.) spoils, armor stripped off a slain enemy
τέκνον, τό, son, child
Τυρρηνικός/Τυρσηνικός, -ή, -όν, Tyrrhenian, Etruscan
ὡς (conj.), (+ subju./opt.) so that, in order that

---

18   πεπλευκότας masc. acc. pl. perf. act. part. < πλέω
20   τήνδ' ἐς Αἰτναίαν πέτραν unlike Homer's *Odyssey*, where the land of the Cyclopes is never specified, in this play (and in later Gk. tradition), they inhabit Sicily

ἵν' οἱ μονῶπες ποντίου παῖδες θεοῦ
Κύκλωπες οἰκοῦσ' ἄντρ' ἔρημ' ἀνδροκτόνοι.
τούτων ἑνὸς ληφθέντες ἐσμὲν ἐν δόμοις
δοῦλοι· καλοῦσι δ' αὐτὸν ᾧ λατρεύομεν
25 Πολύφημον· ἀντὶ δ' εὐίων βακχευμάτων
ποίμνας Κύκλωπος ἀνοσίου ποιμαίνομεν.
παῖδες μὲν οὖν μοι κλειτύων ἐν ἐσχάτοις
νέμουσι μῆλα νέα νέοι πεφυκότες,
ἐγὼ δὲ πληροῦν πίστρα καὶ σαίρειν στέγας
30 μένων τέταγμαι τάσδε, τῷδε δυσσεβεῖ
Κύκλωπι δείπνων ἀνοσίων διάκονος.
καὶ νῦν, τὰ προσταχθέντ', ἀναγκαίως ἔχει
σαίρειν σιδηρᾷ τῇδέ μ' ἁρπάγῃ δόμους,
ὡς τόν τ' ἀπόντα δεσπότην Κύκλωπ' ἐμὸν
35 καθαροῖσιν ἄντροις μῆλά τ' ἐσδεχώμεθα.

---

21 οἱ μονῶπες never described as such by Homer
ποντίου παῖδες θεοῦ in the *Odyssey*, it is implied that only Polyphemus is the child of Poseidon
22 ἄντρ' ἔρημ' = ἄντρα ἔρημα i.e., they are uncivilized since, in the view of most ancient Greeks, they do not live together in a *polis*
23 ἑνὸς either gen. of agent w/ ληφθέντες, i.e. "by...," or gen. of possession w/ δόμοις
ληφθέντες masc. nom. pl. aor. pass. part. < λαμβάνω
26-31 Note *alliteration*
26 ποίμνας...ποιμαίνομεν note *figura etymologica*
27 μοι dat. of interest expressing possession
28 πεφυκότες masc. nom. pl. perf. (= pres.) act. part. < φύω
30 τέταγμαι 1st sing. perf. mid./pass. indic. < τάσσω
32 προσταχθέντ' neut. acc. pl. aor. pass. part. < προστάσσω

ἀναγκαίως (adv.), of necessity, necessarily
ἀνδροκτόνος, -ον, man-killing
ἀνόσιος, -ον, unholy, godless
ἀντί (prep. + gen.), instead
ἄντρον, τό, cave
ἄπειμι, be away or absent
αὐτός, -ή, -ό, (pron. in gen., dat., acc.) him, her, it; (pl.) them
βακχευμάτα, τά, Bacchic revelries
δεῖπνον, τό, principal meal of the day, breakfast-lunch, dinner
δεσπότης, -ου, ὁ, master, lord
διάκονος, ὁ, servant, attendant
δόμος, ὁ, house (pl. often = sing., esp. in verse)
δοῦλος, ὁ, slave
δυσσεβής, -ές, impious, godless
εἷς, μία, ἕν, (gen. ἑνός, μιᾶς, ἑνός), one
εἰσδέχομαι, receive X (acc.) in Y (dat.)
ἐρῆμος, -ον, desolate, lonely, solitary
ἔσχατον, τό, furthest part
εὔιος, -ον, Bacchic (from εὐοῖ, the ecstatic Bacchic cry of joy)
θεός, ὁ, god
ἵνα (adv.), where
καθαρός, -ά, -όν, clean
καλέω, call

κλειτύς, -ύος, ἡ, slope, hillside
Κύκλωψ, -ωπος, ὁ, Cyclops (lit., "Round-eye")
λαμβάνω, seize, take, carry off
λατρεύω, serve, be enslaved to (+ dat.)
μένω, stay (where one is), remain
μῆλον, τό, sheep, goat; (pl.) flocks
μονώψ, -ῶπος, ὁ/ἡ, one-eyed
νέμω, pasture, graze, shepherd
νέος, νέα, νέον, young
οἰκέω, inhabit, dwell, live
ὅς, ἥ, ὅ, who, that, which
οὗτος, αὕτη, τοῦτο, this; (pl.) these
πίστρον, τό, water trough
πληρόω, fill
ποιμαίνω, herd, tend
ποίμνη, ἡ, flock
πόντιος, -α, -ον, of the sea (epithet of Poseidon)
προστάσσω, assign to
σαίρω, sweep, clean
σιδήρεος, -α, -ον, made of iron
στέγη, ἡ, roof; room; (freq. in pl.) house
τάσσω, appoint, assign or order X (acc.) (to do something + inf.)
τε (conj.), and
φύω, bring forth, produce; (perf. and 2nd aor. often =) be

---

32 ἀναγκαίως ἔχει Gk. ἔχω + adv. = English εἰμί + adj.; this is followed by acc. + inf. construction
33 σιδηρᾷ τῇδέ...ἁρπάγῃ dat. of means
35 καθαροῖσιν ἄντροις poetic pl. for sing.
ἐσδεχώμεθα 1st pl. pres. mid./pass. (dep.) subju. < εἰσδέχομαι; subju. in purp. cl. in primary sequence. The 1st pl. either includes his sons or is a bit of pomposity on the part of Silenus (an example of *pluralis maiestatis*)

ἤδη δὲ παῖδας προσνέμοντας εἰσορῶ
ποίμνας. τί ταῦτα; μῶν κρότος σικινίδων
ὅμοιος ὑμῖν νῦν τε χὤτε Βακχίῳ
κῶμος συνασπίζοντες Ἀλθαίας δόμους
40 προσῇτ᾽ ἀοιδαῖς βαρβίτων σαυλούμενοι;

Χορός

παῖ γενναίων μὲν πατέρων
γενναίων δ᾽ ἐκ τοκάδων,
πᾷ δή μοι νίσῃ σκοπέλους;
οὐ τᾷδ᾽ ὑπήνεμος αὔ-
45 ρα καὶ ποιηρὰ βοτάνα;
δινᾶέν δ᾽ ὕδωρ ποταμῶν
ἐν πίστραις κεῖται πέλας ἄντρων, οὗ σοι βλαχαὶ τεκέων.

---

36 προσνέμοντας w/ dir. obj. ποίμνας; sc. this place
37 τί ταῦτα; lit. "What (are) these things?" i.e., "What's going on here?" The satyrs are apparently dancing wildly in a Dionysiac manner and not acting as exhausted shepherds μῶν = μὴ οὖν, "It can't be, can it?"
νῦν τε χὤτε see 2 and note ad loc.
39 κῶμος in *apposition* to the subj. of the vb., i.e., "as a..."
Ἀλθαίας the wife of Oeneus ("Wine-man"), king of Calydon and the first mortal to receive the gift of wine from Dionysus. In at least one account, Althaea slept with Dionysus and had a daughter by him, Deianeira, the wife of Heracles
40 προσῇτ᾽ 2nd pl. imperf. act. < πρόσειμι
41-81 The *parodos* (entrance song), sung by the chorus as it comes onstage for the first time. Note the use of literary Doric (with α substituting for Attic η) throughout

Ἀλθαία, ἡ, Althaea
ἀοιδή, ἡ, song
αὔρα, ἡ, breeze
βάρβιτος, ὁ/ἡ, barbitos (also spelled barbiton; a many-stringed instrument resembling the lyre)
βληχή, ἡ, bleating
βοτάνη, ἡ, fodder
γενναῖος, -α, -ον, noble, well-bred
δή, (particle used to give greater *exactness* to the word or words which it influences) now, in truth, indeed
δινήεις, -εσσα, -εν, eddying
εἰσοράω/εἰσορῶ, see
ἤδη (adv.), now
κεῖμαι, lie, be (in a place)
κρότος, ὁ, beat (of the feet in dancing), rhythmn
κῶμος, ὁ, band of drunken revelers
νίσσομαι/νίσομαι, go (w/ acc. of place)
ὁμοῖος, -α, -ον, same
οὗ (adv.), where

πατήρ, πατέρος/πατρός, ὁ, father
πέλας (adv./prep. + gen.), near
πῆ (interrogative particle), how?
πίστρα, ἡ, trough
ποταμός, ὁ, river
πρόσειμι, approach, go towards (w/ acc. of place)
προσνέμω, drive to or towards
σαυλόομαι, swagger (w/ connotations of lasciviousness)
σίκιννις/σίκινις, -ιδος ἡ, sikinnis (a fast-paced dance of satyrs used in satyr plays)
σκόπελος, peak, headland
συνασπίζω, bear a shield along w/ (+ dat.), support X (dat.)
τε (conj.), and; τε καί/τε...καί, (both)...and
τέκος, -εος, τό, (of animals, esp. in pl.) the young
τῇδε (adv.), this way or direction
τοκάς, -άδος, ἡ, mother
ὕδωρ, ὕδατος, τό, water
ὑπήνεμος, -ον, (lit., under the wind) sheltered from the wind, gentle

---

41 παῖ voc. address to an errant goat or sheep
43 πᾷ = (Doric form of) πῆ
    μοι ethical dat., i.e., "tell me"
    νίσῃ 2nd sing. pres. mid. (dep.) indic. < νίσσομαι
44-5 οὐ...βοτάνα; a negative rhetorical question, expecting a positive response, i.e., "Isn't...?" or "Surely..., isn't it?"
44 τᾷδ' = (Doric form of) τῇδε
45 βοτάνα = (Doric form of) βοτάνη
46 δινᾶέν = (Doric form of) δινῆέν
48 οὗ σοι βλαχαὶ τεκέων sc. εἰσί
    σοι dat. of interest expressing possession (w/ τεκέων)
    βλαχαὶ = (Doric form of) βληχαὶ
    τεκέων = (Epic form of) τεκών

ψύττ᾽· οὐ τᾷδ᾽, οὔ;
50 οὐ τᾷδε νεμῇ κλειτὺν δροσεράν;
ὠή, ῥίψω πέτρον τάχα σου·
ὕπαγ᾽ ὦ ὕπαγ᾽ ὦ κεράστα
μηλοβότα στασιωρὲ
Κύκλωπος ἀγροβάτα.
55 σπαργῶντας μαστοὺς χάλασον·
δέξαι θηλαῖσι τροφὰς
ἃς λείπεις ἀρνῶν θαλάμοις.
ποθοῦσί σ᾽ ἀμερόκοι-
τοι βλαχαὶ σμικρῶν τεκέων.
60 εἰς αὐλὰν πότ᾽ ἀμφιλαφῆ
ποιηροὺς λιποῦσα νομοὺς
Αἰτναίων εἴσει σκοπέλων;
οὐ τάδε Βρόμιος, οὐ τάδε χοροὶ
βακχεῖαί τε θυρσοφόροι,

---

50 νεμῇ 2nd sing. fut. mid. indic. < νέμω
51 σου "at you" (gen. w/ verbs signifying "to aim at")
53 μηλοβότα = (Doric form of) μηλοβότου
54 ἀγροβάτα = (Doric form of) ἀγροβάτου
55 χάλασον 2nd sing. aor. act. impera. < χαλάω
56 δέξαι 2nd sing. aor. mid (dep.). impera. < δέχομαι
56-7 τροφὰς ἃς...ἀρνῶν = τροφὰς ἀρνῶν ἃς i.e., "the (young) brood of lambs that"
57 θαλάμοις dat. of place/locative dat. (common in verse); O'Sullivan and Collard (139) observe that this is: "[a] grandiose expression used by the satyrs...for the cave's interior."

ἀγροβάτης, -ου, ὁ, going through the fields
ἀμφιλαφής, -ές, vast
[ἀρνός], ὁ/ἡ, lamb
αὐλή, ἡ, courtyard
Βακχεῖος, -α, -ον, Bacchic, of or belonging to Bacchus and his rites/worship
δέχομαι, take, accept, receive
δροσερός, -ά, -όν, dewy
ἔρχομαι/εἶμι, go
ἡμερόκοιτος, -ον, sleeping by day
θάλαμος, inner room; (pl. w/ metaphorical sense) pens, folds
θηλή, ἡ, teat
θυρσοφόρος, -ον, thyrsus-bearing
κεράστης, -ου, ὁ, horned (one), i.e., ram
κλειτύς, -ύος, ἡ, slope, hillside
λείπω, ἔλιπον (aor.), leave behind, forsake
μαστός, ὁ, breast; (rarely of animals) udder
μηλοβότης, -ου, ὁ, shepherd
νέμω, pasture, graze; (mid.) feed
νομός, ὁ, pasture
πέτρος, ὁ, stone
ποθέω, long for, miss
ποιηρός, -ή, -όν, grassy
πότε (particle), when?
ῥίπτω, throw
σμικρός, -ά, -όν, small, little
σπαργάω, be full to bursting, swell
στασιωρός, ὁ, watcher or guardian of the sheepfold
τάχα (adv.), quickly, soon
τροφή, ἡ, nourishment, food; nurture, rearing; (here, perhaps, w/ special meaning) brood
ὑπάγω, go on, move forward
χαλάω, let down, unloosen
χορός, ὁ, dance
ψύττα, psst! (hissing sound used to drive a herd on)
ὦ (exclamation), O!, hey!; (voc. marker)
ὠή (exclamation), hey!

58-9 ἀμερόκοιτοι τοι βλαχαὶ σμικρῶν τεκέων lit. "the day-sleeping bleatings of your little children," i.e., "your little bleating children who sleep by day"
ἀμερόκοιτοι = (Doric form of) ἡμερόκοιτοι

60   αὐλάν = (Doric form of) αὐλήν
62   εἴσει 2nd sing. fut. mid. (dep.) < ἔρχομαι/εἶμι
63   οὐ τάδε Βρόμιος lit. "These things (are) not Bromios," i.e., "There's no Dionysus here"
64   θυρσοφόροι "The thyrsus was a long wand or staff, often decorated with ivy (see on 620) or strands of wool, which was carried and waved about by ecstatic worshippers of Dionysus" (Olson, 31)

65   οὐ τυμπάνων ἀλαλαγ-
μοὶ κρήναις παρ' ὑδροχύτοις,
οὐκ οἴνου χλωραὶ σταγόνες·
οὐδ' ἐν Νύσᾳ μετὰ Νυμ-
φᾶν ἴακχον ἴακχον ᾠ-
70   δὰν μέλπω πρὸς τὰν Ἀφροδίταν, ἃν θηρεύων πετόμαν
βάκχαις σὺν λευκόποσιν.
ὦ φίλος ὦναξ Βακχεῖε, ποῖ οἰ-
75   οπολῶν ξανθὰν χαίταν σείεις;
ἐγὼ δ' ὁ σὸς πρόπολος
Κύκλωπι θητεύω
τῷ μονοδέρκτᾳ δοῦλος ἀλαίνων
80   σὺν τᾷδε τράγου χλαίνᾳ μελέᾳ
σᾶς χωρὶς φιλίας.

Σιληνός

σιγήσατ', ὦ τέκν', ἄντρα δ' ἐς πετρηρεφῆ
ποίμνας ἀθροῖσαι προσπόλους κελεύσατε.

---

68   Νύσᾳ = (Doric form of) Νύσῃ
68-9 Νυμφᾶν = (Doric form of) Νυμφῶν
69   ἴακχον in *apposition* to ᾠδὰν
69-70 ᾠδὰν = (Doric form of) ᾠδὴν
70-1 τὰν Ἀφροδίταν = (Doric form of) τὴν Ἀφροδίτην
71   πέτομαι unaugmented Doric form of ἐπετόμην
74   φίλος the nom. can sometimes function as a voc.
      ὦναξ = ὦ ἄναξ
75   ξανθὰν = (Doric form of) ξανθὴν
      χαίταν = (Doric form of) χαίτην
79   μονοδέρκτᾳ = (Doric form of) μονοδέρκτῃ

ἀθροίζω, ἤθροισα (aor.), gather together
ἀλαίνω, wander about
ἀλαλαγμός, ὁ, loud noise, cry
ἄναξ, ἄνακτος, ὁ, lord
Ἀφροδίτη, ἡ, Aphrodite; sex
Βάκχη, ἡ, Bacchant (female follower of Dionysus)
δοῦλος, ὁ, slave
θηρεύω, hunt (after), chase
θητεύω, serve, work for (+ dat.)
ἴακχος, ὁ, Iacchus song (Iacchus was a mystic name of Dionysus originally belonging to an Eleusinian deity)
κελεύω, order, command
κρήνη, ἡ, spring
λευκόπους, -ποδος ὁ/ἡ, white-footed, bare-footed
μέλεος, -α, -ον, wretched
μέλπω, sing
μετά (prep. + gen.), along with, among
μονοδέρκτης, -ου, ὁ, one-eyed
Νῦσα, -ης, ἡ, Nysa (sacred mountain where Dionysus was raised by the local nymphs)
ξάνθη, ἡ, golden
οἶνος, ὁ, wine
οἰοπολέω, roam alone
παρά (prep. + dat.), by, beside

πέτομαι, fly; dart, rush, move quickly
πετρηρεφής, -ές, rock-vaulted, rock-roofed
ποῖ (adv.), where?, to what place?
ποίμνη, ἡ, flock
πρόπολος, ὁ, attendant
πρός (prep. + acc.), to
σείω, shake
σιγάω, be silent
σός, -ή, -όν, your
σταγών, -όνος, ἡ, drop
σύν (prep. + dat.), in the company of, (together) with
τέκνον, τό, child
τράγος, ὁ, he-goat
τύμπανον, τό, kettledrum (used esp. in orgiastic cults such as that of Cybele and Dionysus)
ὑδρόχυτος, -ον, flowing or gushing w/ water
φιλία, ἡ, friendship
φίλος, -η, -ον, dear, beloved
χαίτη, ἡ, loose, flowing hair
χλαῖνα, -ης, ἡ, cloak
χλωρός, -ή, -όν, fresh, sparkling
χωρίς (adv./prep. + gen.), apart from, without
ᾠδή, ἡ, song

---

80   τᾷδε...χλαίνᾳ μελέᾳ = (Doric forms of) τῇδε...χλαίνῃ μελέῃ
81   σᾶς = (Doric form of) σῆς
83   προσπόλους i.e., "your (the Chorus') attendants." These are apparently mute characters who accompany the satyrs on stage and tend to the sheep

Χορός
    χωρεῖτ'· ἀτὰρ δὴ τίνα, πάτερ, σπουδὴν ἔχεις;
Σιληνός
85   ὁρῶ πρὸς ἀκταῖς ναὸς Ἑλλάδος σκάφος
    κώπης τ' ἄνακτας σὺν στρατηλάτῃ τινὶ
    στείχοντας ἐς τόδ' ἄντρον· ἀμφὶ δ' αὐχέσιν
    τεύχη φέρονται κενά, βορᾶς κεχρημένοι,
    κρωσσούς θ' ὑδρηλούς. ὦ ταλαίπωροι ξένοι·
90   τίνες ποτ' εἰσίν; οὐκ ἴσασι δεσπότην
    Πολύφημον οἷός ἐστιν ἄξενόν τε γῆν
    τήνδ' ἐμβεβῶτες καὶ Κυκλωπίαν γνάθον
    τὴν ἀνδροβρῶτα δυστυχῶς ἀφιγμένοι.
    ἀλλ' ἥσυχοι γίγνεσθ', ἵν' ἐκπυθώμεθα
95   πόθεν πάρεισι Σικελὸν Αἰτναῖον πάγον.

---

84   **χωρεῖτ'** addressed to the Chorus' attendants
    τίνα...σπουδὴν ἔχεις i.e., "what's your hurry?" (Olson)
85   **ἀκταῖς** poetic. pl. for sing.
86   **κώπης τ' ἄνακτας** poetic circumlocution for "sailors"
88   **φέρονται** mid.
    κεχρημένοι masc. nom. pl. perf. (= pres.) mid. part. < χράομαι
89   **κρωσσούς θ' ὑδρηλούς** a poetic *tautology*
90   **ἴσασι** 3rd pl. pres. act. indic. < οἶδα
91   **οἷός** sc. of man/person/creature
92   **ἐμβεβῶτες** masc. nom. pl. perf. act. part. < ἐμβαίνω
93   **ἀφιγμένοι** masc. nom. pl. perf. mid. (dep.) part. < ἀφικνέομαι

Αἰτναῖος, -α, -ον, of or belonging to Aetna, Aetnean
ἀκτή, ἡ, shore
ἀμφί (prep. + dat.), around
ἀνδροβρώς, -ῶτος, ὁ/ἡ, man-eating
ἄντρον, τό, cave
ἄξενος, -ον, unfriendly, inhospitable
ἀτάρ (conj.), but
αὐχήν, -ένος, ὁ, neck
ἀφικνέομαι, arrive at, come to (+ acc. in verse)
βορά, ἡ, food
γῆ, ἡ, land, country
γίγνομαι, be; (+ ἥσυχος), keep
γνάθος, ἡ, jaw
δεσπότης, -ου, ὁ, master
δυστυχῶς (adv.), w/ horribly bad luck
ἐκπυνθάνομαι, ἐξεπυθόμην (2nd aor.), learn
Ἑλλάς, -άδος, ἡ, Greece; (adj. w/ a fem. substantive) Greek
ἐμβαίνω, enter upon (+ acc.)
ἔχω, have
ἥσυχος, -ον, quiet, still
ἵνα, (conj.) so that, in order that (+ subju. in secondary sequence)
κενός, -ή, -όν, empty
κρωσσός, ὁ, water jar or jug
Κυκλώπιος, -η, -ον, of the Cyclops, Cyclopean
κώπη, ἡ, oar-handle, oar
ναῦς, ναός, ἡ, ship

ξένος, ὁ, stranger
ὅδε, ἥδε, τόδε, this; (pl.) these
οἶδα, know
οἷος, οἵη, οἷον, what sort, what kind
ὁράω/ὁρῶ, see
πάγος, ὁ, crag, rock
πάρειμι, be present at (+ acc.)
πόθεν (adv.), from where
ποτε (particle), once; (w/ intensive force, in questions) τίς ποτε; 'Who in the world?'
πρός (prep. + dat.), on
Σικελός, -ή, -όν, Sicilian
σκάφος, -εος, τό, hull (of a ship)
σπουδή, ἡ, haste
στείχω, come
στρατηλάτης, -ου, ὁ, general, commander
ταλαίπωρος, -ον, miserable
τε (conj.), and; τε καί/τε...καί, (both)...and
τεῦχος, -εος, τό, vessel, jar, container
τις, τι, (gen. τινος), (indef. adj.), some; any; a certain
τίς, τί (gen. τίνος; interrog. pron. and adj.), who? which? what?
ὑδρηλός, -ή, -όν, for (carrying) water
φέρω, carry
χράομαι, use; (perf. w/ pres. sense) be in need or want of (+ gen.)
χωρέω, move on, go

Ὀδυσσεύς

ξένοι, φράσαιτ' ἂν νᾶμα ποτάμιον πόθεν
δίψης ἄκος λάβοιμεν εἴ τέ τις θέλει
βορὰν ὀδῆσαι ναυτίλοις κεχρημένοις;
⟨ἔα·⟩ τί χρῆμα; Βρομίου πόλιν ἔοιγμεν ἐσβαλεῖν·
100 Σατύρων πρὸς ἄντροις τόνδ' ὅμιλον εἰσορῶ.
χαίρειν προσεῖπον πρῶτα τὸν γεραίτατον.

Σιληνός

χαῖρ', ὦ ξέν'· ὅστις δ' εἶ φράσον πάτραν τε σήν.

Ὀδυσσεύς

Ἴθακος Ὀδυσσεύς, γῆς Κεφαλλήνων ἄναξ.

Σιληνός

οἶδ' ἄνδρα, κρόταλον δριμύ, Σισύφου γένος.

Ὀδυσσεύς

105 ἐκεῖνος αὐτός εἰμι· λοιδόρει δὲ μή.

---

96   φράσαιτ' 2nd pl. aor. act. opt. < φράζω; w/ ἄν, opt. of polite wish, i.e., "could you please..."; the ἄν here also governs λάβοιμεν, though w/ a different function
96-7 νᾶμα ποτάμιον, δίψης ἄκος the grandiloquent phrases are "absurdly pompous in the humble setting." (Seaford, 136)
97   λάβοιμεν 1st pl. aor. act. opt. < λαμβάνω; potential opt.
99-100 Βρομίου, Σατύρων "in emphatic position; "a city of *Dionysus!*", "a mob of *satyrs!*" " (Olson, 33)
99   ἔοιγμεν 1st pl. perf. (= pres.) act. indic. < ἔοικα; English idiom prefers an impersonal vb., i.e., "it seems we..."
     ἐσβαλεῖν English idiom prefers perf. inf. in place of aor.
100 ἄντροις poetic pl. for sing.
101 προσεῖπον so-called dramatic aor., used to denote a state of mind or act indicating a state of mind; trans. as pres.
102 φράσον 2nd sing. aor. act. impera. < φράζω

ἄκος, -εος, τό, cure, relief (+ gen.)
ἀνήρ, ἀνδρός, ὁ, man
αὐτός, -ή, -ό, (intensive adj.) -self; (pl.) –selves; the very one
Βρόμιος, ὁ, (common name/epithet of Dionysus) Roarer (< βρόμιος, -α, -ον, noisy, boisterous)
γένος, -εος/ους, τό, offspring
γεραίτατος, -α, -ον, eldest, oldest
δίψα, -ης, ἡ, thirst
δριμύς, -εῖα, -ύ, piercing, keen, sharp; bitter
ἔα (exclam. of surprise), Whoa!, Hey!
εἰ (conj.), if; whether
εἰσβάλλω/ἐσβάλλω, enter, come upon
εἰσορῶ/ἐσορῶ, see, look at
ἐκεῖνος, -η, -ον, that one, that thing
ἔοικα (perf.), seem (+ inf.)
θέλω, be willing (+ inf.)
Ἰθακος, ὁ, the Ithacan, i.e., person (or hero) from Ithaca
Κεφαλλῆνες, οἱ, the Cephallenians (collective designation of the subjects of Odysseus on islands and mainland near Ithaca)

κρόταλον, τό, rattle, castanet (used in the worship of Cybele or Dionysus)
λαμβάνω, take (as)
λοιδορέω, abuse, revile
νᾶμα, -ατος, τό, running water, stream, current
ναυτίλος, ὁ, sailor
ὀδάω, sell
ὅμιλος, ὁ, crowd, throng, mob
ὅστις, ἥτις, ὅ τι, (in indir. question) who, what
πάτρα, ἡ, fatherland, native country
πόθεν (adv.), from which? where?
πόλις, πόλιος/πόλεως, ἡ, city, city-state
ποτάμιος, -α, -ον, of or from a river
προσεῖπον (aor.), speak to, address; + τινὰ χαίρειν, bid someone greeting(s)
πρῶτα (neut. pl. acc. adj. as adv.), first
Σίσυφος, ὁ, Sisyphus
φράζω, point out, indicate
χαίρω, rejoice, be glad; (impera. used as greeting) hello! good-bye!; (inf. used as noun of greeting) welcome, greetings
χρῆμα, -ατος, τό, thing, matter; w/ τί, an intensified question: "What is this?"

---

104 κρόταλον δριμύ i.e., "a wheedling chatterer" (Kovacs), "a shrill, relentless babbler" (O'Sullivan and Collard)
Σισύφου γένος Sisyphus, a king of Corinth, was infamous as the most cunning of men. In some traditions he impregnated Anticleia, Odysseus' mother, before her marriage to Laertes, Odysseus' father
105 λοιδόρει...μή = μή λοιδόρει sc. με

Σιληνός
πόθεν Σικελίαν τήνδε ναυστολῶν πάρει;
Ὀδυσσεύς
ἐξ Ἰλίου γε κἀπὸ Τρωϊκῶν πόνων.
Σιληνός
πῶς; πορθμὸν οὐκ ᾔδησθα πατρῴας χθονός;
Ὀδυσσεύς
ἀνέμων θύελλαι δεῦρό μ' ἥρπασαν βίᾳ.
Σιληνός
110 παπαῖ· τὸν αὐτὸν δαίμον' ἐξαντλεῖς ἐμοί.
Ὀδυσσεύς
ἦ καὶ σὺ δεῦρο πρὸς βίαν ἀπεστάλης;
Σιληνός
λῃστὰς διώκων οἳ Βρόμιον ἀνήρπασαν.
Ὀδυσσεύς
τίς δ' ἥδε χώρα καὶ τίνες ναίουσί νιν;
Σιληνός
Αἰτναῖος ὄχθος Σικελίας ὑπέρτατος.
Ὀδυσσεύς
115 τείχη δὲ ποῦ 'στι καὶ πόλεως πυργώματα;
Σιληνός
οὐκ ἔστ'· ἔρημοι πρῶνες ἀνθρώπων, ξένε.

---

106 πόθεν...πάρει cf. 95
107 An example of *hendiadys* (Gk. "one through two"), the use of two separate words or phrases to refer to a single thing (here = "the Trojan War")
κἀπὸ = καὶ ἀπὸ
108 πῶς; i.e., "How (is it that you ended up here)?"

ἀναρπάζω, kidnap, carry off
ἄνεμος, ὁ, wind
ἄνθρωπος, ὁ, person, human
ἀποστέλλω, send off or away; (pass.) go away, be sent off course
ἁρπάζω, snatch away, carry off
βία, ἡ, force, violence; (dat. sing. as adv.) w/ force, violently; πρὸς βίαν, "against one's will"
γε (enclitic particle, giving emphasis to the word or words which it follows. With single words, "at least," "at any rate," but often only to be rendered by italics in writing, or emphasis in pronunciation)
δαίμων, -ονος, ὁ/ἡ, divine power, (good or ill) fortune, fate
δεῦρο (adv.), here, to this place
διώκω, pursue
ἐξαντλέω/ἐξαντλῶ, endure
ἐρῆμος, -ον, empty, void, or destitute of (+ gen.)
ἦ (adv.), Can it be? Is it true?
θύελλα, ἡ, squall, furious storm
Ἴλιος, ἡ, Ilium (i.e., Troy)

λῃστής, -οῦ, ὁ, pirate
ναίω, inhabit, dwell in
ναυστολέω, sail, go by ship
νιν (Doric and Tragic acc. 3rd pers. sing. pron. = αὐτόν, αὐτήν)
ὅς, ἥ, ὅ, who, that, which
ὄχθος, ὁ, mound, hill
παπαῖ (colloquial cry of surprise), Damn! (or similar)
πατρῷος, -α, -ον, of one's father
πόνος, ὁ, trouble, suffering
πορθμός, ὁ, passage to (+ gen.)
ποῦ (adv.), where?
πρών, πρῶνος, ὁ, headland
πύργωμα, -ατος, τό, fortified city; (pl.) fortifications, battlements
πῶς (adv.), how?
Σικελία, ἡ, Sicily
τεῖχος, -εος, τό, wall, city-wall
Τρωϊκός, -ή, -όν, Trojan
ὑπέρτατος, -η, -ον, highest
χθών, χθονός, ἡ, land, country
χώρα, ἡ, country, land, place

---

108 ᾔδησθα 2nd sing. pluperf. (= imperf.) act. < οἶδα
110 τὸν αὐτὸν in the attributive position, αὐτός, -ή, -ό = "the same"
    ἐμοί dat. of comparison (Gk. = "to me"; English = "as me")
111 ἀπεστάλης 2nd sing. aor. pass. indic. < ἀποστέλλω
113 τίς δ' ἥδε χώρα sc. ἐστι
115 τείχη...'στι...πυργώματα neut. pl. subj. (x2) take sing. vb.
    'στι = ἐστι
116 ἔρημοι πρῶνες ἀνθρώπων = πρῶνες (sc. ἐστὶ) ἔρημοι ἀνθρώπων

Ὀδυσσεύς

τίνες δ' ἔχουσι γαῖαν; ἦ θηρῶν γένος;

Σιληνός

Κύκλωπες, ἄντρ' οἰκοῦντες, οὐ στέγας δόμων.

Ὀδυσσεύς

τίνος κλύοντες; ἦ δεδήμευται κράτος;

Σιληνός

120 μονάδες· ἀκούει δ' οὐδὲν οὐδεὶς οὐδενός.

Ὀδυσσεύς

σπείρουσι δ' — ἦ τῷ ζῶσι; — Δήμητρος στάχυν;

Σιληνός

γάλακτι καὶ τυροῖσι καὶ μήλων βορᾷ.

Ὀδυσσεύς

Βρομίου δὲ πῶμ' ἔχουσιν, ἀμπέλου ῥοάς;

Σιληνός

ἥκιστα· τοιγὰρ ἄχορον οἰκοῦσι χθόνα.

Ὀδυσσεύς

125 φιλόξενοι δὲ χὥσιοι περὶ ξένους;

Σιληνός

γλυκύτατά φασι τὰ κρέα τοὺς ξένους φορεῖν.

Ὀδυσσεύς

τί φῄς; βορᾷ χαίρουσιν ἀνθρωποκτόνῳ;

118-28 Cf. Silenus' description of the Euripidean Cyclopes' way of life with that of Odysseus' description in *Od.* 9.107-15

118 στέγας δόμων i.e., houses w/ roofs

119 τίνος κλύοντες sc. εἰσι

δεδήμευται 3rd sing. perf. pass. indic. < δημεύω; "Athens was in this period a vigorous democracy [δημοκρατία], and

ἀκούω, heed, pay attention to, or obey X (gen.) about Y (acc.)
ἄμπελος, ἡ, grape-vine
ἀνθρωποκτόνος, -ον, homicidal; (furnished by) murdered/slaughtered men
ἄντρον, τό, cave
ἄχορος, -ον, w/out dances (i.e., joyless)
βορά, ἡ, meat
γαῖα, ἡ, land
γάλα, γάλακτος, τό, milk
γένος, -ους, τό, race
γλυκύτατος, -α, -ον, most delicious
δημεύω, make public, turn over to the people
Δημήτηρ, -τρος, ἡ, Demeter
δόμος, ὁ, house
ἔχω, have, hold, occupy, inhabit
ζάω/ζῶ, ἡ, live
ἤ (conj.), or
ἦ (adv.), Is it perhaps? Can it be?
ἥκιστα (neut. pl. acc. adj. as adv.), least of all, not at all
θήρ, θηρός, ὁ, wild beast
κλύω, listen to, obey (+ gen.)
κράτος, -εος, τό, power

κρέας, τό, (pl. κρέα), meat, piece of meat
μῆλον, τό, sheep, goat; (pl.) flocks
μονάς, -άδος, ἡ, solitary
οἰκέω, inhabit, dwell, live
ὅσιος, -α, -ον, pious, god-fearing
οὐδείς, οὐδεμία, οὐδέν, no one, nobody, nothing
περί (prep. + acc.), w/ regard to
πῶμα, -ατος, τό, drink
ῥοή/ῥοά, ἡ, stream
στάχυς, -υος, (acc. στάχυν), ὁ, grain, wheat
στέγη, ἡ, roof, roofed place; (often in pl. =) house, dwelling
σπείρω, sow
τυρός, ὁ, cheese
τοιγάρ (inferential particle), therefore, as a consequence
φημί, say
φιλόξενος, -ον, hospitable (towards strangers)
φορέω, have, possess
χαίρω, rejoice at, take delight in (+ dat.)

Euripides' 5th-century Odysseus naturally assumes that the Cyclopes may have a similar form of government." (Olson, 35)

120 μονάδες sc. εἰσι
οὐδὲν οὐδεὶς οὐδενός Gk., unlike English, allows double (and triple) negatives in formal speech
121 σπείρουσι...στάχυν an example of *hyperbaton*
τῷ = (alternative form of) τίνι; dat. of means
122 γάλακτι... τυροῖσι...βορᾷ; dat. of means; sc. ζῶσι
125 φιλόξενοι cf. *Od.* 9.174-6
χὤσιοι = καὶ ὅσιοι

Σιληνός
 οὐδεὶς μολὼν δεῦρ' ὅστις οὐ κατεσφάγη.
Ὀδυσσεύς
 αὐτὸς δὲ Κύκλωψ ποῦ 'στιν; ἦ δόμων ἔσω;
Σιληνός
130 φροῦδος, πρὸς Αἴτνῃ θῆρας ἰχνεύων κυσίν.
Ὀδυσσεύς
 οἶσθ' οὖν ὃ δρᾶσον, ὡς ἀπαίρωμεν χθονός;
Σιληνός
 οὐκ οἶδ', Ὀδυσσεῦ· πᾶν δέ σοι δρῴημεν ἄν.
Ὀδυσσεύς
 ὅδησον ἡμῖν σῖτον, οὗ σπανίζομεν.
Σιληνός
 οὐκ ἔστιν, ὥσπερ εἶπον, ἄλλο πλὴν κρέας.
Ὀδυσσεύς
135 ἀλλ' ἡδὺ λιμοῦ καὶ τόδε σχετήριον.
Σιληνός
 καὶ τυρὸς ὀπίας ἔστι καὶ βοὸς γάλα.
Ὀδυσσεύς
 ἐκφέρετε· φῶς γὰρ ἐμπολήμασιν πρέπει.
Σιληνός
 σὺ δ' ἀντιδώσεις, εἰπέ μοι, χρυσὸν πόσον;
Ὀδυσσεύς
 οὐ χρυσὸν ἀλλὰ πῶμα Διονύσου φέρω.

---

128 μολών masc. nom. sing. aor. act. part. < βλώσκω
κατεσφάγη 3rd. sing. aor. pass. indic. < κατασφάζω; a gnomic aor. expressing a general truth; translate as a pres.

Αἴτνη, ἡ, Mt. Aetna
ἀλλός, -ή, -ό, another, other
ἀντιδίδωμι, give in return
ἀπαίρω, depart from (+ gen.)
βλώσκω, go, come
βοῦς, βοός, ὁ/ἡ, cow
δράω, do
εἴσω/ἔσω (adv.; prep. + gen.), within
ἐκφέρω, bring out
ἐμπόλημα, -ατος, τό, freight or cargo of a ship; (pl.) wares, merchandise
ἡδύς, ἡδεῖα, ἡδύ, pleasant
ἰχνεύω, hunt
κατασφάζω, murder, slaughter
κύων, κυνός, ὁ/ἡ, dog
λέγω, εἶπον (aor.), say, speak
λιμός, ὁ, hunger
ὀδάω, sell
ὅδε, ἥδε, τόδε, this; (pl.) these
ὀπίας, ὁ, (w/ or w/out τυρός) cheese made from milk curdled w/ fig-juice (ὀπός)
ὅστις, ἥτις, ὅ τι, who, which
πᾶς, πᾶσα, πᾶν, all, every
πλήν (prep. + gen.), except
πόσος, -η, -ον, how much?
πρέπει, is fitting or proper
πρός (prep. + dat.), on
σῖτος, ὁ, bread
σπανίζω, lack, be in need of (+ gen.)
σχετήριον, τό, check or remedy against (+ gen.)
φέρω, bring, carry
φροῦδος, -η, -ον, (of persons) gone away
φῶς, φωτός τό, light
χρυσός, ὁ, gold
ὡς (conj.), so that, in order that (+ subju. in primary sequence)
ὥσπερ (adv.), just as

---

129 δόμων poetic pl. for sing.
    δόμων ἔσω means little more than "at home"; prep. ἔσω can follow the word it governs (an example of *anastrophe*)
130 φροῦδος sc. ἐστι
    θῆρας ἰχνεύων κυσίν the Cyclops is portrayed as an aristocrat who possesses the wealth and leisure to go hunting. In contrast, Homer's less civilized Cyclops has no dogs
    κυσίν dat. of means
131 οἶσθ'...ὃ δρᾶσον "lit. "do you know (the thing) which—do it!", i.e., "do you know what you need to do?"... Colloquial." (Olson, 36)
    ἀπαίρωμεν 1st pl. pres. act. subj. < ἀπαίρω; subju. in purp. cl.
132 δρῴημεν 1st pl. pres. act. opt. < δράω; potential opt.
135 ἡδύ...σχετήριον = τόδε καὶ (ἐστὶ) ἡδὺ σχετήριον λιμοῦ
136 ὀπίας fig-juice acted as a curdling agent
138 ἀντιδώσεις 2nd sing. fut. act. indic. < ἀντιδίδωμι

Σιληνός

140 ὦ φίλτατ' εἰπών, οὗ σπανίζομεν πάλαι.

Ὀδυσσεύς

καὶ μὴν Μάρων μοι πῶμ' ἔδωκε, παῖς θεοῦ.

Σιληνός

ὃν ἐξέθρεψα ταῖσδ' ἐγώ ποτ' ἀγκάλαις;

Ὀδυσσεύς

ὁ Βακχίου παῖς, ὡς σαφέστερον μάθῃς.

Σιληνός

ἐν σέλμασιν νεώς ἐστιν, ἢ φέρεις σύ νιν;

Ὀδυσσεύς

145 ὅδ' ἀσκὸς ὃς κεύθει νιν, ὡς ὁρᾷς, γέρον.

Σιληνός

οὗτος μὲν οὐδ' ἂν τὴν γνάθον πλήσειέ μου.

Ὀδυσσεύς

⟨τοῦτον μὲν οὖν τὸν ἀσκὸν οὐκ ἂν ἐκπίοις.⟩

Σιληνός

⟨φύει γὰρ ἀσκὸς οἶνον ἐξ αὐτοῦ πάλιν;⟩

Ὀδυσσεύς

ναί, δὶς τόσον πῶμ' ὅσον ἂν ἐξ ἀσκοῦ ῥυῇ.

Σιληνός

καλήν γε κρήνην εἶπας ἡδεῖάν τ' ἐμοί.

---

141 Cf. *Od.* 9.197-207
καὶ μήν "(Yes,) and moreover" (the phrase is used to introduce something new or special)
ἔδωκε 3rd sing. aor. act. indic. < δίδωμι
θεοῦ i.e., Dionysus. In the *Odyssey*, Maron is the child of Εὐάνθης

ἀγκάλη, ἡ, bent arm
ἀσκός, ὁ, wine-skin
Βάκχιος/Βάκχος, ὁ, Bacchus (common name/epithet of Dionysus)
γέρων, -οντος, ὁ, old man
γνάθος, ἡ, jaw
δίδωμι, give
δίς (adv.), twice
ἑαυτοῦ, -ῆς, -οῦ, (reflex. pron. in oblique cases) himself, herself, itself
ἐκπίνω, drink X (acc.) dry
ἐκτρέφω, ἐξέθρεψα, bring up, raise from childhood
καλός, -ή, -όν, fine, beautiful, lovely
κεύθω, contain
κρήνη, ἡ, spring
μανθάνω, learn
Μάρων, -ωνος, ὁ, Maron
ναί (adv.), yes!
ναῦς, νεώς, ἡ, ship

νιν (Doric and Tragic acc. 3rd pers. sing. pron. = αὐτόν, αὐτήν)
οἶνος, ὁ, wine
ὁράω/ὁρῶ, see
ὅσος, -η, -ον, as much as
παῖς, παιδός, ὁ, son, child
πάλαι (adv.), for a long time now
πάλιν (adv.), again, once more, anew
πίμπλημι, fill, fill up
ποτε (particle), once
ῥέω, flow
σαφέστερον (adv.), more clearly
σέλμα, -ατος, τό, upper planking (of a ship); (pl.) deck
τόσος, -η, -ον, so much
φίλτατα (adv.), in a manner most pleasing
φύω, produce, bring forth
ὡς (conj.), so that, in order that (+ subju. in primary sequence); (adv.) as

---

142   ἀγκάλαις dat. pl. of ἀγκάλη, w/ or w/out ἐν, = "in..."
143   μάθῃς 2nd sing. aor. act. subju. < μανθάνω; subju. in purp. cl. in primary sequence
     γνάθον i.e., my mouth
146   μέν note the lack of a corresponding δέ cl., which would be something like "but a larger skin would!"
     πλήσειέ 3rd sing. aor. act. opt. < πίμπλημι; potential opt.
     ⟨τοῦτον...πάλιν;⟩ editors posit that two verses have dropped out of the text at this point. The supplements are courtesy of Kovacs
     ἐκπίοις 2nd sing. aor. act. opt. < ἐκπίνω; potential opt.
     αὑτοῦ = (Attic contraction of) ἑαυτοῦ
147   ῥυῇ 3rd sing. aor. act. subju. < ῥέω; generalizing subju. after ὅσον, i.e., "as much as (ever)..."
148   εἶπας the aor. here seems to indicate action just past; translate as pres.

Ὀδυσσεύς

βούλῃ σε γεύσω πρῶτον ἄκρατον μέθυ;

Σιληνός

150 δίκαιον· ἦ γὰρ γεῦμα τὴν ὠνὴν καλεῖ.

Ὀδυσσεύς

καὶ μὴν ἐφέλκω καὶ ποτῆρ' ἀσκοῦ μέτα.

Σιληνός

φέρ' ἐγκάναξον, ὡς ἀναμνησθῶ πιών.

Ὀδυσσεύς

ἰδού.

Σιληνός

παπαιάξ, ὡς καλὴν ὀσμὴν ἔχει.

Ὀδυσσεύς

εἶδες γὰρ αὐτήν;

Σιληνός

οὐ μὰ Δί', ἀλλ' ὀσφραίνομαι.

Ὀδυσσεύς

155 γεῦσαί νυν, ὡς ἂν μὴ λόγῳ 'παινῇς μόνον.

---

149 βούλῃ...γεύσω βούλομαι often precedes a deliberative subju.: lit., "do you want...should/am I...?" English idiom prefers "do you want me to..."

150 δίκαιον sc. ἐστι

151 ἀσκοῦ μέτα prep. μετά can follow the word it governs, in which case its accent falls back onto the first syllable (an example of *anastrophe*)

152 φέρ' impera. of φέρω is often used as adv., "come," "now," "come on now," esp. before another impera. (a colloquial usage)

ἄκρατος, -ον, unmixed (i.e., undiluted w/ water), neat
ἀναμιμνήσκω, remind; (pass.) remember
βούλομαι, want, wish
γεῦμα, -ατος, τό, taste
γεύω, give X (acc.) a taste of Y (acc.) [the double acc. is unique to this passage]; (mid.) taste, have a taste of
δίκαιος, -α, -ον, fair, reasonable
ἐγκανάσσω, pour in (wine)
ἐπαινέω, praise
ἐφέλκω, draw behind, have in tow (i.e., bring along)
ἔχω, have
Ζεύς, Διός, Διΐ, Δία, ὁ, Zeus
ἦ (adv.), in truth, truly
καλέω, invite
λόγος, ὁ, speech
μά, (particle used in protestations and oaths, + acc. of person/god sworn by) by
μέθυ, -υος, τό, wine
μετά (prep. + gen.), with
μόνον (adv.), only, alone
νυν (adv.), then
ὀσμή, ἡ, smell, scent, bouquet
παπαιάξ, (comic-colloquial expression of surprise)
πίνω, ἔπιον (aor.), drink
ποτήρ, -ῆρος, ὁ, drinking cup
πρῶτον (adv.), first
ὠνή, ἡ, buying, purchasing; purchase
ὡς (conj.), so that, in order that (+ subju. in primary sequence); (adv.) how!, what a!

---

152 ἀναμνησθῶ 1st sing. aor. pass. subju. < ἀναμιμνήσκω; subju. in purp. cl. in primary sequence. Silenus claims that it has been so long since he has tasted wine that he has forgotten what the experience is like

153 ἰδού impera. of εἶδον ("look!" < ὁράω/ὁρῶ) is often used as adv., "there you are!" (a colloquial usage)

154 εἶδες γὰρ αὐτήν this seemingly strange question is prompted by Silenus' description of the wine's smell as καλή, since that adj. normally is applied to physical appearances
γάρ "(are you saying this) because...?" (Olson)

155 γεῦσαί 2nd sing. mid. aor. impera. < γεύω
λόγῳ dat. of means
'παινῇς 2nd sing. pres. act. subju. < ἐπαινέω; subju. in purp. cl. (w/ rare inclusion of modal particle ἄν) in primary sequence

Σιληνός
   βαβαί· χορεῦσαι παρακαλεῖ μ' ὁ Βάκχιος.
   ἆ ἆ ἆ.
Ὀδυσσεύς
   μῶν τὸν λάρυγγα διεκάναξέ σου καλῶς;
Σιληνός
   ὥστ' εἰς ἄκρους γε τοὺς ὄνυχας ἀφίκετο.
Ὀδυσσεύς
160 πρὸς τῷδε μέντοι καὶ νόμισμα δώσομεν.
Σιληνός
   χάλα τὸν ἀσκὸν μόνον· ἔα τὸ χρυσίον.
Ὀδυσσεύς
   ἐκφέρετέ νυν τυρεύματ' ἢ μήλων τόκον.
Σιληνός
   δράσω τάδ', ὀλίγον φροντίσας γε δεσποτῶν.
   ὡς ἐκπιεῖν κἂν κύλικα βουλοίμην μίαν,
165 πάντων Κυκλώπων ἀντιδοὺς βοσκήματα,
   ῥῖψαι τ' ἐς ἄλμην Λευκάδος πέτρας ἄπο
   ἅπαξ μεθυσθεὶς καταβαλών τε τὰς ὀφρῦς.

156-7 "Dancing was about as important to satyrs as drinking, and for them, there can hardly be one without the other." (O'Sullivan and Collard, 148)
158 μῶν = (adv.; contraction of) μὴ οὖν, "surely not?"; here used ironically
159 ὥστ' + indic. = real result
   ἄκρους γε τοὺς ὄνυχας i.e., the very tips of my toe/finger nails
161 ἔα i.e., "never mind" (Kovacs) or "to hell with" (Olson)
163 δεσποτῶν if this doesn't refer to masters in general (see

ἆ (exclamation)
ἄκρος, -α, -ον, outermost
ἄλμη, ἡ, brine; sea
ἅπαξ (adv.), just once
ἀφικνέομαι, ἀφικόμην, arrive at (+ εἰς)
βαβαί (exclamation of surprise or amazement)
βόσκημα, -ατος, τό, that which is fed or fatted; (pl.) sheep, goats, cattle
βούλομαι, wish, want (+ inf.)
διακανάσσω, gurgle through
δίδωμι, δώσω, give
δράω, do
ἐάω, let be, let alone
εἷς, μία, ἕν, (gen. ἑνός, μιᾶς, ἑνός), one
ἐκπίνω, ἐξέπιον, drink X (acc.) dry
καλῶς (adv.), nicely
καταβάλλω, κατέβαλον, let fall or drop
κύλιξ, -ικος, ἡ, wine cup
λάρυγξ, -υγγος, ὁ, larynx; (poetic) throat

Λευκάς, Λευκάδος, ἡ, Leucas
μεθύσκω, make drunk
μέντοι (particle; μέν + τοι), furthermore, moreover
μῆλον, τό, sheep, goat; (pl.) flocks
νόμισμα, -ατος, τό, money
ὀλίγον (adv.), little, slightly
ὄνυξ, -υχος, ὁ, finger or toe nail
ὀφρύς, -ύος, (pl. acc. ὀφρῦς), ἡ, eyebrow
παρακαλέω, summon; call, invite
πέτρα, ἡ, rock (frequently of cliffs, ledges, etc. by the sea)
πρός (prep. + dat.), in addition to
ῥίπτω, throw, cast, or hurl oneself
τόκος, τό, young, offspring
τύρευμα, -ατος, τό, cheese (lit., "that which is curdled")
φροντίζω, take thought, pay heed
χαλάω, loosen, undo (things drawn tightly together)
χορεύω, dance (w/ joy), take part in the chorus
χρυσίον, τό, gold, gold coin, money
ὡς (conj.), since

---

165), then it is possibly the so-called pl. of majesty, normally used in verse to grant dignity to the sing.

164 κἂν = καὶ ἄν
βουλοίμην 1st sing. pres. dep. opt. < βούλομαι; potential opt.
165 ἀντιδούς masc. nom. sing. aor. act. part. < ἀντιδίδωμι
166 Λευκάδος πέτρας ἄπο ἀπό can follow the word it governs, in which case its accent falls back onto the first syllable (*anastrophe*). From this island's white (= Λευκάς) limestone cliffs, criminals were thrown to their deaths
167 μεθυσθεὶς masc. nom. sing. aor. pass. part. < μεθύσκω
καταβαλών τε τὰς ὀφρῦς i.e., "relaxing my furrowed eyebrows" (O'Sullivan and Collard), i.e., "looking happy." Silenus' brow is furrowed because of his sufferings

ὡς ὅς γε πίνων μὴ γέγηθε μαίνεται·
ἵν' ἔστι τουτί τ' ὀρθὸν ἐξανιστάναι
170 μαστοῦ τε δραγμὸς καὶ παρεσκευασμένου
ψαῦσαι χεροῖν λειμῶνος ὀρχηστύς θ' ἅμα
κακῶν τε λῆστις. εἶτ' ἐγὼ <οὐ> κυνήσομαι
τοιόνδε πῶμα, τὴν Κύκλωπος ἀμαθίαν
κλαίειν κελεύων καὶ τὸν ὀφθαλμὸν μέσον;

Χορός
175 ἄκου', Ὀδυσσεῦ· διαλαλήσωμέν τί σοι.

Ὀδυσσεύς
καὶ μὴν φίλοι γε προσφέρεσθε πρὸς φίλον.

Χορός
ἐλάβετε Τροίαν τὴν Ἑλένην τε χειρίαν;

Ὀδυσσεύς
καὶ πάντα γ' οἶκον Πριαμιδῶν ἐπέρσαμεν.

---

168 γέγηθε 3rd sing. perf. (= pres.) act. indic. < γηθέω; lit., "(has rejoiced and therefore) is happy/does rejoice"
169 ἔστι "it is possible" (+ inf.)
τουτί more emphatic than τοῦτο, this deictic ("pointing out") form of the demonstrative indicates that Silenus is "grab[bing], or at least point[ing] to, his phallus, a conspicuous part of the satyric actor's costume." (O'Sullivan and Collard, 154)
ἐξανιστάναι pres. act. inf. < ἐξανίστημι
170 μαστοῦ τε δραγμὸς sc. where there is
170-1 παρεσκευασμένου...λειμῶνος "as λειμών connotes moisture as well as fertility (LSJ s.v. I), then the participle may refer to lubrication, natural or otherwise, in preparation for sex." (O'Sullivan and Collard, 154)
171 χεροῖν dual, dat. of means
ὀρχηστύς θ' ἅμα sc. where there is

ἀκούω, listen
ἅμα (adv.), at the same time
γηθέω, rejoice
διαλαλέω, talk or discuss w/ X (dat.) about Y (acc.)
δραγμός, ὁ, grasping, fondling
εἶτα (adv.), and so, then, therefore
Ἑλένη, ἡ, Helen
ἐξανίστημι, make X (acc.) rise up/stand to attention
ἵνα (adv.), where, when
κακά, τά, cares, troubles, woes
κλαίω, cry, wail
κυνέω, κυνήσομαι (dep. fut.), kiss
λαμβάνω, ἔλαβον, seize, capture, take, take hold of
λειμών, -ῶνος, ὁ, any moist, grassy place, meadow; (here metaphorically referring to a woman's genitals)
λῆστις, -εως, ἡ, forgetting, forgetfulness
μαίνομαι, be mad or crazy

μαστός, ὁ, woman's breast
οἶκος, ὁ, house
ὀρθός, -ή, -όν, upright, erect
ὀρχηστύς, -ύος, ἡ, dancing
παρασκευάζω, make ready
πᾶς, πᾶσα, πᾶν, entire, whole
πέρθω, ἔπερσα, sack
Πριαμίδης, -ου, ὁ, son of Priam (patronymic of the last king of Troy)
τις, τι, (gen. τινος), (indef. pron.) anyone, anything; someone, something; (indef. adj.) some, a certain
τοιόσδε, -άδε, -όνδε, such as this
Τροία, ἡ, Troy
προσφέρω, bring to; (pass.) go to or towards, approach
φίλος, ὁ, friend
χείρ, χειρός, ἡ, hand
χείριος, -α, -ον, in one's hand, i.e., captive
ψαύω, touch X (gen.)

---

173 τὴν Κύκλωπος ἀμαθίαν grandiloquent periphrasis; lit., "the ignorance of the Cyclops," i.e., "that idiot Cyclops"

174 κλαίειν i.e., "to be damned" (Olson), "to go to hell" (O'Sullivan and Collard); κλαίειν κελεύων is a colloquialism, lit. "ordering him to cry or wail"
μέσον predicative, i.e., "in the middle of (his forehead)"

175 διαλαλήσωμέν 1st pl. aor. act. subju. < διαλαλέω; hortatory subju., but best translated in English as a purp. cl.

176 καὶ μὴν "Yes indeed!" (Olson), "Of course" (Kovacs); the phrase is used to introduce something new or special
φίλοι γε "since as friends"; φίλοι is in *apposition* to the pronominal 2nd pl. ending of προσφέρεσθε (which is either impera. or indic., though the latter is prob. more likely here)

Χορός

οὔκουν, ἐπειδὴ τὴν νεᾶνιν εἵλετε,
180 ἅπαντες αὐτὴν διεκροτήσατ' ἐν μέρει,
ἐπεί γε πολλοῖς ἥδεται γαμουμένη,
τὴν προδότιν; ἣ τοὺς θυλάκους τοὺς ποικίλους
περὶ τοῖν σκελοῖν ἰδοῦσα καὶ τὸν χρύσεον
κλῳὸν φοροῦντα περὶ μέσον τὸν αὐχένα
185 ἐξεπτοήθη, Μενέλεων, ἀνθρώπιον
λῷστον λιποῦσα. μηδαμοῦ γένος ποτὲ
φῦναι γυναικῶν ὤφελ', εἰ μὴ 'μοὶ μόνῳ.

Σιληνός

ἰδού· τάδ' ὑμῖν ποιμνίων βοσκήματα,
ἄναξ Ὀδυσσεῦ, μηκάδων ἀρνῶν τροφαί,
190 πηκτοῦ γάλακτός τ' οὐ σπάνια τυρεύματα.

---

179 τὴν νεᾶνιν i.e., Helen
182-4 τοὺς θυλάκους...τὸν αὐχένα i.e., Paris, Helen's lover/ new husband, "who is imagined dressing like a wealthy 5th-century Persian." (Olson, 40). Note the *double entendres*
183 τοῖν σκελοῖν dat. dual
184 κλῳὸν "a deliberately nasty term for a necklace" (Olson, 40)
185 ἐξεπτοήθη 3rd sing. aor. pass. indic. < ἐκπτοέω
ἀνθρώπιον dim., here w/ pejorative force
186-7 μηδαμοῦ...ὤφελ' "would that the race of women were (φῦναι aor. act. inf. < φύω) nowhere ever (i.e., nonexistent)"
187 εἰ μὴ 'μοὶ μόνῳ sc. to have sex with
188 ἰδού impera. of εἶδον "'look!" < ὁράω/ὁρῶ) is often used as adv., "there you are," "(look) here" (a colloquial usage)
188-90 τάδ'...τυρεύματα sc. ἐστι/εἰσι
190 οὐ σπάνια an example of *litotes*: "not a few" = "a large number of"

αἱρέω, εἷλον (aor.), seize
ἄναξ, ἄνακτος, ὁ, lord
ἀνθρώπιον, τό, little person (diminutive of ἄνθρωπος)
ἅπας, ἅπασα, ἅπαν, quite all, the whole; (pl.) all together
[ἀρνός], ὁ, lamb, sheep
αὐχήν, -ένος, ὁ, neck; (comic use) penis
γάλα, γάλακτος, τό, milk
γαμέω, marry, take to wife; (mid.) (of the woman) give herself in marriage to, get married to (+ dat.)
γένος, -ους, τό, race
γυνή, γυναικός, ἡ, woman
διακροτέω, knock a hole through; (comic use) fuck hard, bang
εἰ (conj.), if; + μή, "except"
ἐκπτοέω, stun w/ amazement
ἐπεί (conj.), since, seeing that
ἐπειδή (conj.), when
ἥδομαι, enjoy, take pleasure in (+ nom. part.)
θύλακος, ὁ, pouch, wallet; (pl.) pants or trousers worn by the Persians (which were never worn by Greeks); (cognate θυλάκη means "scrotum")
κλῳός, ὁ, dog-collar
λείπω, ἔλιπον, leave behind, forsake
λῷστος, -η, -ον, very or most desirable, agreeable; very good

Μενέλεως, -εω, ὁ, Menelaos
μέρος, -εος, τό, (one's) turn
μέσος, -η, -ον, middle (of)
μηδαμοῦ (adv.), nowhere
μηκάς, μηκάδος, ἡ, the bleating one
μόνος, -η, -ον, alone
νεᾶνις, -ιδος, ἡ, girl
ὁράω/ὁρῶ, εἶδον, see
οὔκουν (adv.), isn't it the case that?
ὀφείλω, be bound or obliged; (imperf. and aor. are often used, followed by inf., to express a wish that cannot be accomplished) would that...
περί (prep. + dat./acc.), around
πηκτός, -ή, -όν, curdled
ποικίλος, -η, -ον, many-colored, embroidered
ποίμνιον, τό, flock
πολύς, πολλή, πολύ, much; (pl.) many
ποτε (particle), ever
προδότις, -ιδος, ἡ, traitor
σκέλος, -εος, τό, leg
σπάνιος, -η, -ον, few
τροφή, ἡ, nurture, rearing; (poetic) nursling, young animal
φορέω, wear
φύω, bring forth, produce; (perf. and sometimes 2nd aor. often =) be
χρύσεος, -η, -ον, gold, golden

φέρεσθε· χωρεῖθ' ὡς τάχιστ' ἄντρων ἄπο,
βότρυος ἐμοὶ πῶμ' ἀντιδόντες εὐίου.
οἴμοι· Κύκλωψ ὅδ' ἔρχεται· τί δράσομεν;
Ὀδυσσεύς
ἀπολώλαμέν τἄρ', ὦ γέρον· ποῖ χρὴ φυγεῖν;
Σιληνός
195 ἔσω πέτρας τῆσδ', οὗπερ ἂν λάθοιτέ γε.
Ὀδυσσεύς
δεινὸν τόδ' εἶπας, ἀρκύων μολεῖν ἔσω.
Σιληνός
οὐ δεινόν· εἰσὶ καταφυγαὶ πολλαὶ πέτρας.
Ὀδυσσεύς
οὐ δῆτ'· ἐπεί τἂν μεγάλα γ' ἡ Τροία στένοι,
εἰ φευξόμεσθ' ἕν' ἄνδρα, μυρίον δ' ὄχλον
200 Φρυγῶν ὑπέστην πολλάκις σὺν ἀσπίδι.

---

191 **φέρεσθε** impera. addressed to Odysseus and his men
 ὡς τάχιστ' (ὡς + superl. adv. = "super superl."), "as quickly as possible"
 ἄντρων ἄπο for the position of ἀπό, see 166
 ἀντιδόντες masc. nom. pl. aor. act. part. < ἀντιδίδωμι
194 **ἀπολώλαμέν** 1st pl. perf. (= pres.) act. indic. < ἀπόλλυμι
 τἄρ' = τοι ἄρα
195-6 **ἔσω πέτρας τῆσδ'...ἀρκύων**, ἔσω note *chiasmus*
195 **ἂν λάθοιτέ γε** "'you might at least (γε) escape notice," i.e., if not get away altogether" (Olson, 41)
 λάθοιτέ 2nd pl. aor. act. opt. < λανθάνω; potential opt.
196 **δεινὸν τόδ' εἶπας** = τόδ' is a δεινὸν that εἶπας; for εἶπας as = pres., see 148 note
 μολεῖν aor. act. inf. < βλώσκω
197 **καταφυγαὶ...πέτρας** i.e., hiding places in the rock
198 **οὐ δῆτ'** emphatic denial, i.e., "I shall not do it." (Kovacs)

ἀνήρ, ἀνδρός, ὁ, man
ἀντιδίδωμι, give in return
ἄντρον, τό, cave
ἀπόλλυμι, destroy utterly; (perf. act.) be done for, be lost
ἄρα (particle), then, as it seems
ἄρκυς, -υος, ἡ, hunter's net
ἀσπίς, -ίδος ἡ, shield
βλώσκω, go
βότρυς, -υος, ὁ, bunch of grapes, grape-cluster
γέρων, -οντος, ὁ, old man
δεινός, -ή, -όν, frightful, dangerous, terrible
δῆτα (adv.), (more emphatic form of δή, "in truth," "indeed")
εἷς, μία, ἕν, (gen. ἑνός, μιᾶς, ἑνός), one
εἴσω/ἔσω (adv.; prep. + gen.), within, into
ἔρχομαι, come
εὔιος, -ον, Bacchic (from εὐοῖ, the ecstatic Bacchic cry of joy)
καταφυγή, ἡ, place of refuge
μεγάλα (adv.), loudly
μυρίος, -α, -ον, countless
ὅδε, ἥδε, τόδε, this; (pl.) these
οἴμοι (exclamation of pain, fright, pity, anger, grief, or surprise)

ὄχλος, ὁ, crowd, throng
πέτρα, ἡ, rock (frequently of cliffs, ledges, etc. by the sea)
ποῖ (adv.), where?, to what place?
πολλάκις (adv.), many times, often
πῶμα, -ατος, τό, drink
οὗπερ (adv.), (the very place) where
Φρύξ, Φρυγός, ὁ, Phrygian (an inhabitant of the region around Troy in classical times, and thus often used as a poetic equivalent of 'Trojan')
στένω, groan
σύν (prep. + dat.), with
τάχιστα (adv.), very/most quickly
τίς, τί (gen. τίνος; interrog. pron. and adj.), who? which? what?
τοι (particle), let me tell you (in English, usu. conveyed by means of emphasis or tone)
ὑφίστημι, place or set under; (2nd aor. act.) resist, withstand
φεύγω, φεύξομαι, ἔφυγον, flee
χωρέω, move on, go
χρή, it is necessary, one must (+ inf.)

198-202 Odysseus, forgetting that he is no longer in the heroic world of Homeric epic, "rehearses the heroic code of standing one's grounds against the enemy" (O'Sullivan and Collard, 158)

198-9 An "emotional" fut. condit. (a type of FMV), of a thing not desired, w/ a potential opt. in place of the fut. indic. in the apodosis

τἄν = τοι ἄν

στένοι 3rd sing. pres. act. opt.

200 ὑπέστην 1st sing. aor. act. indic. < ὑφίστημι

ἀλλ', εἰ θανεῖν δεῖ, κατθανούμεθ' εὐγενῶς
ἢ ζῶντες αἶνον τὸν πάρος συσσώσομεν.

Κύκλωψ

ἄνεχε πάρεχε· τί τάδε; τίς ἡ ῥᾳθυμία;
τί βακχιάζετ'; οὐχὶ Διόνυσος τάδε,
205 οὐ κρόταλα χαλκοῦ τυμπάνων τ' ἀράγματα.
πῶς μοι κατ' ἄντρα νεόγονα βλαστήματα;
ἦ πρός τε μαστοῖς εἰσι χὐπὸ μητέρων
πλευρὰς τρέχουσι, σχοινίνοις τ' ἐν τεύχεσιν
πλήρωμα τυρῶν ἐστιν ἐξημελγμένον;
210 τί φατε; τί λέγετε; τάχα τις ὑμῶν τῷ ξύλῳ
δάκρυα μεθήσει. βλέπετ' ἄνω καὶ μὴ κάτω.

---

201   θανεῖν aor. act. inf. < θνήσκω
      κατθανούμεθ' = (syncopated form of) καταθανούμεθ',
      1st. pl. fut. dep. indic. < καταθνήσκω
202   αἶνον τὸν πάρος "our reputation, the one we formerly
      had," i.e., as brave warriors
203   ἄνεχε πάρεχε lit., "rise up, allow"; apparently formulaic,
      prob. = something like "Get out of the way, make way!"
      (O'Sullivan and Collard)
      τί τάδε; τίς ἡ ῥᾳθυμία; sc. ἐστι to each question
204   οὐχὶ Διόνυσος τάδε lit. "These things (are) not
      Dionysus," i.e., "There's no Dionysus here" (and cf. 63)
205   κρόταλα χαλκοῦ τυμπάνων τ' ἀράγματα note
      chiasmus
206   μοι dat. of feeling (aka, ethical dat.), i.e., "tell me," but
      also expressing possession, i.e., "my νεόγονα βλαστήματα"
207-8 πρός τε μαστοῖς...τρέχουσι an example of *hysteron
      proteron*
      εἰσι, τρέχουσι pl. vbs. can be used w/ neut. pl. nouns
      (νεόγονα βλαστήματα) that describe living things
207   χὐπὸ = καὶ ὑπό; ὑπό governs πλευρὰς

αἶνος, ὁ, reputation
ἄνω (adv.), up
ἄραγμα, -ατος, τό, rattling, clattering
βακχιάζω, ἡ, act like a worshipper of Dionysus
βλάστημα, -ατος, τό, offspring
βλέπω, look
δάκρυον, τό, tear
δεῖ, it is necessary (+ inf.)
ἐξαμέλγω, press or squeeze out
εὐγενῶς (adv.), nobly
κάτω (adv.), down
ζάω/ζῶ, live
ἤ (conj.), or
ἦ (interrogative adv.)
θνήσκω, die
κατά (prep. + acc.), (down) in, throughout
καταθνήσκω, die
κρόταλον, τό, rattle, castanet (used in the worship of Cybele or Dionysus)
λέγω, say
μαστός, ὁ, breast; (rarely of animals) udder, teat

μεθίημι, let fall
μήτηρ, μητρός, ἡ, mother
νεόγονος, ον, new-born
ξύλον, τό, club
πάρος (adv.), formerly
πλευρά, ἡ, side
πλήρωμα, -ατος, τό, total amount, full load
πρός (prep. + dat.), at
πῶς (adv.), how?
ῥᾳθυμία, ἡ, relaxation, carefree behavior; laziness
συσσώζω, retain, preserve (lit. "save together w/ one's life")
σχοίνινος, -η, -ον, made of rushes
τάχα (adv.), quickly, soon
τεῦχος, εος, τό, vessel
τρέχω, run
τύμπανον, τό, kettledrum (used esp. in orgiastic cults such as that of Cybele and Dionysus)
τυρός, ὁ, cheese
ὑπό (prep. + acc.), under
φημί, say
χαλκός, ὁ, bronze

---

208 σχοινίνοις τ' ἐν τεύχεσιν i.e., the baskets "in which freshly made cheese was placed to dry after it had been pressed to remove most of the whey (cf. 209)." (Olson, 42)

209 ἐστιν ἐξημελγμένον 3rd sing. perf. pass. (periphrastic ἐστι(ν)+ perf. pass. part.) indic. < ἐξαμέλγω

210 φατε, λέγετε synonymous vbs. expressing the Cyclops' growing impatience at the lack of response on the satyrs' part

τῷ ξύλῳ dat. of means; i.e., "courtesy of..." (O'Sullivan and Collard) or "as a result of being beaten with..." (Olson)

211 μεθήσει 3rd sing. fut. act. indic. < μεθίημι
βλέπετ' ἄνω καὶ μὴ κάτω i.e., look at me when I'm talking to you (the satyrs, cowering in fear, are avoiding eye contact w/ the Cyclops, who towers above them)

Χορός
  ἰδού· πρὸς αὐτὸν τὸν Δί' ἀνακεκύφαμεν
  τά τ' ἄστρα, καὶ τὸν Ὠρίωνα δέρκομαι.
Κύκλωψ
  ἄριστόν ἐστιν εὖ παρεσκευασμένον;
Χορός
215 πάρεστιν. ὁ φάρυγξ εὐτρεπὴς ἔστω μόνον.
Κύκλωψ
  ἦ καὶ γάλακτός εἰσι κρατῆρες πλέῳ;
Χορός
  ὥστ' ἐκπιεῖν γέ σ', ἢν θέλῃς, ὅλον πίθον.
Κύκλωψ
  μήλειον ἢ βόειον ἢ μεμιγμένον;
Χορός
  ὃν ἂν θέλῃς σύ· μὴ 'μὲ καταπίῃς μόνον.

---

212 πρὸς αὐτὸν τὸν Δί' i.e., in the direction of the sky
  ἀνακεκύφαμεν 1st pl. perf. act. indic. < ἀνακύπτω
212-13 ἀνακεκύφαμεν...δέρκομαι note mixture of pl. and sing., "appropriate in the mouth of a Choragus ["Chorus Leader"], who speaks both as an individual member of the Chorus, and also as its representative." (Long, 15)
213 Ὠρίωνα both a giant and the constellation he becomes post-mortem. Though it is not night, the chorus "are simply pretending to mistake the Cyclops for Orion" (Waterfield, 153) in both of his manifestations. "The Orion reference is apt for the Euripidean Polyphemus.... Both are club-wielding giants and sons of Poseidon...; both are violent and lecherous,.... Both meet with the same punishment [i.e., blinding]." (O'Sullivan and Collard, 159)

ἀνακύπτω, lift up one's head
ἄριστον, τό, lunch
ἄστρον, τό, star
αὐτός, -ή, -ό, (intensive adj.) -self; (pl.) -selves
βόειος, -α, -ον, of a cow
δέρκομαι, see
ἐκπίνω, ἐξέπιον (aor.), drink X (acc.) dry
εὖ (adv.), well
εὐτρεπής, -ές, ready
Ζεύς, Διός, Διΐ, Δία, ὁ, Zeus
ἦ (adv.), Can it be? Is it true?
θέλω, wish
καταπίνω, gulp or swallow down
κρατήρ, -ῆρος, ὁ, mixing bowl (in which wine was mixed w/ water)
μήλειος, -ον, of sheep
μίγνυμι, mix
μόνον (adv.), only
ὅλος, -η, -ον, whole, entire
ὅς, ἥ, ὅ, who, that, which
παρασκευάζω, prepare
πάρειμι, be ready or at hand
πίθος, ὁ, a large storage jar (on average 4-6 feet in height)
πλέως, πλέα, πλέων, full of, filled w/ (+ gen.)
φάρυγξ, φάρυγ(γ)ος, ὁ, throat, gullet
Ὠρίων, -ωνος, ὁ, Orion
ὥστε (conj.), (+ inf. = a potential result) so that

---

214 ἐστιν...παρεσκευασμένον 3rd sing. perf. pass. (periphrastic ἐστι(ν) + perf. pass. part.) indic. < παρασκευάζω
215 ἔστω 3rd sing. pres. act. impera. < εἰμί
216-17 "Both κρατήρ and πίθος are more appropriate for wine than milk." (Seaford, 147)
216 πλέῳ masc. nom. pl.
217 ὥστ' "(they are indeed full), so that..."
ἦν = εἰ ἄν (+ subju.) = protasis of a FMV (general) condit.
218 μήλειον ἢ βόειον sc. ἐστὶ τὸ γάλα
μεμιγμένον neut. nom. sing. perf. mid./pass. part. < μίγνυμι; Greeks almost never drank cow's milk, but barbarians (i.e., non-Greeks) did. When Greeks did drink milk, which was rare, they preferred that of goats or sheep. For Polyphemus to employ the word "mixed" characterizes him comically (since milk is involved) as both a barbarian and as an overly sophisticated aristocrat—a truly ridiculous combination in the eyes of a fifth-century BCE Athenian audience
219 καταπίῃς 2nd sing. aor. act. subju. < καταπίνω; prohibitive subju.

Κύκλωψ

220 ἥκιστ'· ἐπεί μ' ἂν ἐν μέσῃ τῇ γαστέρι
πηδῶντες ἀπολέσαιτ' ἂν ὑπὸ τῶν σχημάτων.
ἔα· τίν' ὄχλον τόνδ' ὁρῶ πρὸς αὐλίοις;
λῃσταί τινες κατέσχον ἢ κλῶπες χθόνα;
ὁρῶ γέ τοι τούσδ' ἄρνας ἐξ ἄντρων ἐμῶν
225 στρεπταῖς λύγοισι σῶμα συμπεπλεγμένους,
τεύχη τε τυρῶν συμμιγῆ γέροντά τε
πληγαῖς μέτωπον φαλακρὸν ἐξῳδηκότα.

Σιληνός

ὤμοι, πυρέσσω συγκεκομμένος τάλας.

Κύκλωψ

ὑπὸ τοῦ; τίς ἐς σὸν κρᾶτ' ἐπύκτευσεν, γέρον;

Σιληνός

230 ὑπὸ τῶνδε, Κύκλωψ, ὅτι τὰ σ' οὐκ εἴων φέρειν.

---

220 ἥκιστ' i.e., "Don't worry about *that*!" (Olson)
220-1 ἂν...ἂν repetition of the modal particle has no effect on the sentence's meaning
221 ἀπολέσαιτ' 2nd pl. aor. act. opt. < ἀπόλλυμι; potential opt.
αὐλίοις pl. for sing. if the first two definitions are intended
224 ὁρῶ γέ τοι note the force of the particles: "I *do* see, at any rate..."
225 στρεπταῖς λύγοισι dat. of means; the same noun is used in *Od.* 9.427, where Odysseus employs withes to tie together groups of three sheep (along w/ one of his men under the middle sheep) in order to escape from the Cyclops' cave the next morning
σῶμα acc. of respect; sing. for pl.
συμπεπλεγμένους masc. acc. pl. perf. mid./pass. part. < συμπλέκω

ἄντρον, τό, cave
ἀπόλλυμι, destroy utterly
[ἀρνός], ὁ/ἡ, lamb
αὔλιον, τό, cottage; cave; fold, pen
γαστήρ, -έρος, ἡ, belly
ἔα (exclam. of surprise), Whoa!, Hey!
ἐάω, allow
ἐξοιδέω, swell
ἐπεί (conj.), since, seeing that
ἥκιστα (adv.), least of all, not at all
κατέχω, κατέσχον, put into shore, land; occupy, seize
κλώψ, κλωπός, ὁ, thief
κράς, κρατός, τό, head
λῃστής, -οῦ, ὁ, pirate
λύγος, ἡ, the *Vitex agnus-castus* tree, also known as the 'chaste tree'; (pl. =) twigs or withes (of this tree, which are similar to those of the willow)
μέσος, -η, -ον, middle (of)
μέτωπον, τό, forehead, head

ὁράω/ὁρῶ, see
ὅτι (particle), because
ὄχλος, ὁ, crowd, throng
πηδάω, leap, spring, bound
πληγή, ἡ, blow
πυκτεύω, strike w/ the fist (+ ἐς, 'on/against')
πυρέσσω, be feverish, have a fever
στρεπτός, -ή, -όν, twisted
συγκόπτω, beat up
συμμιγής, -ές, mixed up together
συμπλέκω, tie or bind together
σχῆμα, -ατος, τό, form, figure; (pl.) dance moves
τάλας, τάλαινα, τάλαν, suffering, wretched
τίς, τί (gen. τίνος; interrog. pron. and adj.), who? which? what?
ὑπό (prep. + gen.), by
φαλακρός, -ά, όν, bald
φέρω, carry off as plunder, steal
χθών, χθονός, ἡ, land, country
ὤμοι (exclamation of surprise, joy, or pain)

226-7 γέροντά...ἐξῳδηκότα "the Cyclops here misdiagnoses the effect of the wine on Silenus, who them improvises his story to agree with the Cyclops' mistake." (Kovacs, 89)
227 πληγαῖς dat. of means
μέτωπον φαλακρόν accs. of respect
ἐξῳδηκότα masc. acc. sing. perf. act. part. < ἐξοιδέω
228 συγκεκομμένος masc. nom. sing. perf. mid./pass. part. < συγκόπτω
229 τοῦ = τίνος
230 τὰ σ' lit., "your things," i.e., "your property"
εἴων 1st sing. imperf. act. < ἐάω

Κύκλωψ
οὐκ ἦσαν ὄντα θεόν με καὶ θεῶν ἄπο;
Σιληνός
ἔλεγον ἐγὼ τάδ'· οἱ δ' ἐφόρουν τὰ χρήματα,
καὶ τόν τε τυρὸν οὐκ ἐῶντος ἤσθιον
τούς τ' ἄρνας ἐξεφοροῦντο· δήσαντες δὲ σὲ
235 κλῳῷ τριπήχει κατὰ τὸν ὀφθαλμὸν μέσον
τὰ σπλάγχν' ἔφασκον ἐξαμήσεσθαι βίᾳ,
μάστιγί τ' εὖ τὸ νῶτον ἀπολέψειν σέθεν,
κἄπειτα συνδήσαντες ἐς θἀδώλια
τῆς ναὸς ἐμβαλόντες ἀποδώσειν τινὶ
240 πέτρους μοχλεύειν, ἢ 's μυλῶνα καταβαλεῖν.

---

231 ἦσαν 3rd pl. pluperf. (= imperf.) act. indic. < οἶδα
θεῶν ἄπο i.e., descended from gods
233 ἐφόρουν the imperf. of this frequentative form of φέρω here has conative force, i.e., "they kept trying to..."; so too ἐξεφοροῦντο in 234
οὐκ ἐῶντος sc. ἐμοῦ ; gen. abs.
235 κλῳῷ τριπήχει dat. of means; collars, usu. made of wood, were put on mischievous dogs and criminals; thus "Silenus' fiction tries to convey to Polyphemus that the strangers view him as bestial as well as criminal" (O'Sullivan and Collard); a cubit is the distance from one's elbow to the tip of one's extended finger (i.e., about 18 inches/46 cm)
κατὰ τὸν ὀφθαλμὸν μέσον lit., "in (sight of) your eye, (the one) in the middle of (your foreheard)," i.e., "as you watch" (Olson)
236 ἐξαμήσεσθαι fut. mid. inf. < ἐξαμάω
βίᾳ dat. of means; so too μάστιγί in 237
237 σέθεν = σου

ἀποδίδωμι, ἀποδώσω, sell (as a slave), deliver over
ἀπολέπω, flay
βία, ἡ, force
δέω, bind, tie, enchain
ἐδώλιον, τό, seat; (pl.) raised quarter-deck (at the stern)
ἐκφορέω, carry out; (mid.) take out w/ one
ἐμβάλλω, ἐνέβαλον, throw in
ἐξαμάω, mow out; (mid.) cut or scrape out
ἔπειτα (adv.), then
ἐσθίω, eat
θεός, ὁ, god
κατά (prep. + acc.), in the sight of
καταβάλλω, κατέβαλον, throw (down)
κλοιός, ὁ, collar (for dogs and criminals)
λέγω, say, speak, tell
μάστιξ, -ιγος, ἡ, whip, scourge
μοχλεύω, move X (acc.) w/ a lever
μυλών, -ῶνος, ὁ, mill
ναῦς, ναός, ἡ, ship
νῶτον, τό, back
οἶδα, know
ὀφθαλμός, ὁ, eye
πέτρος, ὁ, stone, boulder
σπλάγχνα, τά, entrails, guts
συνδέω, bind or tie together
τις, τι, (gen. τινος), (indef. pron.) anyone, anything; someone, something
τρίπηχυς, -υ, three cubits wide or long
φάσκω, say
φορέω, (continually) carry off
χρῆμα, -ατος, τό, thing; (pl.) goods, property

---

238   κἄπειτα = καί ἔπειτα
      συνδήσαντες sc. you (i.e., the Cyclops) as obj.; so too w/ ἐμβαλόντες, ἀποδώσειν, and καταβαλεῖν in the following two lines; note *asyndeton* w/ the participles
      θἀδώλια = τὰ ἑδώλια
240   πέτρους μοχλεύειν since Cyclopes were famous as builders of Bronze Age citadels (cf. esp. the "Cyclopean" walls of Mycenae and Tiryns), "putting Polyphemus to work in a quarry seems to be a grim joke on the abilities of Cyclopes as builders of monumental architecture" (O'Sullivan and Collard, 161)
      'ς μυλῶνα καταβαλεῖν "Grain was ground by hand, and to be thrown into a commercial mill was an extraordinarily cruel fate, since the work was not only exhausting but endless." (Olson, 44). How a disemboweled person (236) could even survive, let alone be expected to perform such physically demanding labor is, of course, part of the absurdity of Silenus' lies and of Satyric drama in general

Κύκλωψ
ἄληθες; οὔκουν κοπίδας ὡς τάχιστ' ἰὼν
θήξεις μαχαίρας καὶ μέγαν φάκελον ξύλων
ἐπιθεὶς ἀνάψεις; ὡς σφαγέντες αὐτίκα
πλήσουσι νηδὺν τὴν ἐμὴν ἀπ' ἄνθρακος
245 θερμὴν διδόντες δαῖτα τῷ κρεανόμῳ,
τὰ δ' ἐκ λέβητος ἐφθὰ καὶ τετηκότα.
ὡς ἔκπλεώς γε δαιτός εἰμ' ὀρεσκόου·
ἅλις λεόντων ἐστί μοι θοινωμένῳ
ἐλάφων τε, χρόνιος δ' εἴμ' ἀπ' ἀνθρώπων βορᾶς.

Σιληνός
250 τὰ καινά γ' ἐκ τῶν ἠθάδων, ὦ δέσποτα,
ἥδιόν' ἐστίν. οὐ γὰρ οὖν νεωστί γε
ἄλλοι πρὸς οἴκους σοὺς ἀφίκοντο ξένοι.

Ὀδυσσεύς
Κύκλωψ, ἄκουσον ἐν μέρει καὶ τῶν ξένων.

241-2 οὔκουν... θήξεις fut. vb. + οὐ = urgent impera.
241 ὡς τάχιστ' (ὡς + superl. adv. = "super superl."), "as quickly as possible"
ἰὼν masc. nom. sing. pres. act. part. < ἔρχομαι/εἶμι
242-3 μέγαν φάκελον ξύλων ἐπιθεὶς sc. hearth
ἐπιθεὶς masc. nom. sing. aor. act. part. < ἐπιτίθημι
244-6 Cf. Homer's Polyphemus, who only ate his victims raw
244 ἀπ' ἄνθρακος i.e., after they have been roasted on the coals
246 τὰ δ'...τετηκότα the entire line is a second dir. obj. of διδόντες; w/ τὰ, sc. κρέα (neut. pl.), "(prepared) meat"
τετηκότα neut. acc. pl. perf. act. part. < τήκω

ἀκούω, listen to (+ gen.)
ἄληθες (adv.), is that so?, really?
ἅλις (adv.), enough of (+ gen.)
ἀλλός, -ή, -ό, other
ἀνάπτω, light
ἄνθραξ, -ακος, ὁ, charcoal
αὐτίκα (adv.), at once
ἀφικνέομαι, ἀφικόμην, arrive
βορά, ἡ, food
δαίς, δαιτός, ἡ, meal, food
δεσπότης, -ου, ὁ, master
δίδωμι, give
ἐκ (prep. + gen.), after
ἔκπλεως, -ων, quite or completely full of (+ gen.)
ἔλαφος, ὁ/ἡ, deer
ἐπιτίθημι, place or put on
ἔρχομαι/εἶμι, go
ἐφθός, -ή, -όν, boiled
ἡδίων, ἥδιον, more pleasant
ἠθάς, -άδος, customary, usual
θερμός, -ή, -όν, hot
θήγω, sharpen, whet
θοινάω, entertain; (mid.) feast, feast on
καινός, -ή, -όν, new

κοπίς, -ίδος, ἡ, chopper, cleaver, broad curved knife
κρεανόμος, ὁ, one who divides up or carves the meat
λέβης, -ητος, ὁ, cauldron
λέων, -οντος, ὁ, lion
μάχαιρα, large knife (used for carving meat)
μέγας, μεγάλη, μέγα, big, large
μέρος, -εος, τό, (one's) turn
νεωστί (adv.), recently, lately
νηδύς, -ύος, ἡ, stomach, belly
ξένος, ὁ, stranger
ξύλον, τό, wood, firewood
οἶκος, ὁ, house
ὀρεσκόος, -ον, mountain-bred, wild
οὔκουν (adv.), not therefore?, not then?, and so not?
πίμπλημι, πλήσω, fill
σφάζω, ἐσφάγην (aor. pass.), slaughter (by cutting the throat)
τήκω, melt; (perf. act.) be made tender
φάκελος, ὁ, bundle
χρόνιος, -α, -ον, for a long time
ὡς (conj.), since

---

247   ἔκπλεώς i.e., tired of eating
ἅλις λεόντων ἐστί μοι θοινωμένῳ lit., "it is enough of lions to me feasting," i.e., "I've had enough of feasting on lions"

249   χρόνιος δ' εἴμ' ἀπ' i.e., "it's been a long time since I had any..." (Olson, 45)
ἀνθρώπων βορᾶς lit., "food consisting of human beings"

250   γ' "marks assent...to Polyphemus' explanation of his eagerness for human flesh (247-9)" (Olson, 46)
οἴκους pl. for sing.

ἡμεῖς βορᾶς χρῄζοντες ἐμπολὴν λαβεῖν
255 σῶν ἆσσον ἄντρων ἤλθομεν νεὼς ἄπο.
τοὺς δ' ἄρνας ἡμῖν οὗτος ἀντ' οἴνου σκύφου
ἀπημπόλα τε κἀδίδου πιεῖν λαβὼν
ἑκὼν ἑκοῦσι, κοὐδὲν ἦν τούτων βίᾳ.
ἀλλ' οὗτος ὑγιὲς οὐδὲν ὧν φησιν λέγει,
260 ἐπεί κατελήφθη σοῦ λάθρᾳ πωλῶν τὰ σά.
Σιληνός
ἐγώ; κακῶς γ' ἄρ' ἐξόλοι'.
Ὀδυσσεύς
εἰ ψεύδομαι.
Σιληνός
μὰ τὸν Ποσειδῶ τὸν τεκόντα σ', ὦ Κύκλωψ,
μὰ τὸν μέγαν Τρίτωνα καὶ τὸν Νηρέα,
μὰ τὴν Καλυψὼ τάς τε Νηρέως κόρας,
265 μὰ θαἰερὰ κύματ' ἰχθύων τε πᾶν γένος,
ἀπώμοσ', ὦ κάλλιστον ὦ Κυκλώπιον,

---

254 βορᾶς...ἐμπολὴν λαβεῖν lit., "to take merchandise consisting of food," i.e., "to purchase food"
255 κἀδίδου = καὶ ἐδίδου
258 ἑκὼν ἑκοῦσι lit., "a willing person to willing people," i.e., both parties entered into this transaction willingly
βίᾳ dat. of means; i.e., no violence was involved
259 ὧν grammatically, one expects the acc. pl. (ἅ) as rel. pron., but Gk. rel. prons. often keep the case of their antecedents (τούτων)
260 κατελήφθη 3rd sing. aor. pass. indic. < καταλαμβάνω
τὰ σά see 230
261 ἐξόλοι' 2nd sing. aor. mid. opt. < ἐξόλλυμι; opt. of wish
εἰ ψεύδομαι sc. "might I indeed perish horribly"

ἀντί (prep. + gen.), at the price of, for, in exchange for
[ἀρνός], ὁ, lamb, sheep
ἀπεμπολάω, sell
ἀπόμνυμι, ἀπώμοσα, deny on oath (often w/ redundant neg. and inf. of action denied)
ἄρα (particle), in that case, then
ἆσσον (adv./prep. + gen.), very near, near
γένος, -ους, τό, race
ἑκών, ἑκοῦσα, ἑκόν, willing
ἐμπολή, ἡ, merchandise, purchase
ἐξόλλυμι, destroy utterly; (mid.) perish utterly
ἐπεί (conj.), since, seeing that
ἔρχομαι, ἦλθον, come
ἱερός, -ά, -όν, holy
ἰχθύς, -ύος, ὁ, fish
κακῶς (adv.), miserably, horribly
κάλλιστος, -η, -ον, very/most, fine, good, or handsome (in, Attic often added to a name in token of love or admiration)

Καλυψώ, -οῦς, ἡ, Calypso
καταλαμβάνω, catch
κόρη, ἡ, daughter
κῦμα, -ατος, τό, wave
λάθρη (adv./prep. + gen.), w/out the knowledge of, unknown to, in secret from (+ gen.)
λαμβάνω, ἔλαβον, take
μά, (particle used in oaths), by
ναῦς, νεώς, ἡ, ship
Νηρεύς, -έως, ὁ, Nereus
οὐδείς, οὐδεμία, οὐδέν, no one, nobody, nothing
οὗτος, αὕτη, τοῦτο, this; (pl.) these
Ποσειδῶν, -ῶνος, (acc. -ῶ), ὁ, Poseidon
πωλέω, exchange or barter goods, sell
σκύφος, ὁ, cup
τίκτω, ἔτεκον, beget
Τρίτων, -ωνος, ὁ, Triton
ὑγιής, -ές, sound, true
φημί, say
χρῄζω, desire (+ inf.)

262-5 When swearing oaths, Greeks often included more than one divinity in the belief that invoking several gods would be more effective. After the mention of three important sea deities (Poseidon [god of the sea and Polyphemus' father],Triton [Poseidon's son and "second-in-command," Nereus [an ancient sea-divinity]), the list—even before the comical absurdity of 265—descends into parody w/ the naming of Calypso (famous for keeping Odysseus on her island for seven years, and not a sea-divinity at all) and Nereus' daughters (he had fifty), who, w/ the exception of Thetis, mother of Achilles, were rather insignificant deities

265 θαἱερά = τὰ ἱερά

266 ἀπώμοσ' "aor. is often used w/ vbs. of swearing to mark the speaker's absolute resolution." (Olson, 47)
Κυκλώπιον dim. of Κύκλωψ, here w/ affectionate force

ὦ δεσποτίσκε, μὴ τὰ σ' ἐξοδᾶν ἐγὼ
ξένοισι χρήματ'. ἢ κακῶς οὗτοι κακοὶ
οἱ παῖδες ἀπόλοινθ', οὓς μάλιστ' ἐγὼ φιλῶ.

Χορός

270 αὐτὸς ἔχ'. ἔγωγε τοῖς ξένοις τὰ χρήματα
περνάντα σ' εἶδον· εἰ δ' ἐγὼ ψευδῆ λέγω,
ἀπόλοιθ' ὁ πατήρ μου· τοὺς ξένους δὲ μὴ ἀδίκει.

Κύκλωψ

ψεύδεσθ'· ἔγωγε τῷδε τοῦ Ῥαδαμάνθυος
μᾶλλον πέποιθα καὶ δικαιότερον λέγω.
275 θέλω δ' ἐρέσθαι· πόθεν ἐπλεύσατ', ὦ ξένοι;
ποδαποί; τίς ὑμᾶς ἐξεπαίδευσεν πόλις;

Ὀδυσσεύς

Ἰθακήσιοι μὲν τὸ γένος, Ἰλίου δ' ἄπο,
πέρσαντες ἄστυ, πνεύμασιν θαλασσίοις
σὴν γαῖαν ἐξωσθέντες ἥκομεν, Κύκλωψ.

---

267 δεσποτίσκε dim. of δεσπότης, here w/ affectionate force
μὴ redundant neg. after ἀπώμοσ'
ἐξοδᾶν pres. act. inf. < ἐξοδάω; governed by ἀπώμοσ', i.e., "I deny on oath that I was selling"
ἐγὼ note the force of the pron.: "I deny on oath that I was selling your possessions, *I* (sc. swear that this is the case)"
268 ἢ "or (if I am lying/this isn't true)," "otherwise"
268-9 κακῶς...ἀπόλοινθ' a multi-layered joke, for: (1) "Satyrs are immortal..., so this wish is destined to remain unfulfilled... The fact that he at least ostensibly puts his sons' lives on the line with this false oath and calls them κακοί ('miserable') undercuts any claims he makes to feeling affection for them as he does here." (O'Sullivan and Collard, 164-5); (2) "One would normally expect the person issuing an oath to demand his *own* destruction if he is lying,

ἀδικέω, do wrong to
ἀπόλλυμι, destroy utterly; (mid.) perish utterly, die
ἄστυ, -εως, τό, city
γαῖα, ἡ, land
δικαιότερος, -α, -ον, more righteous, just, or honest
ἐγώγε, strengthend form of ἐγώ
ἐκπαιδεύω, bring up from childhood
ἐξωθέω, drive forth
ἔρομαι, ask
ἥκω, have come to, be present at
θαλάσσιος, -α, -ον, of, in, on, or from the sea
θέλω, wish
Ἰθακήσιος, -α, -ον, Ithacan
κακός, -ή, -όν, miserable, worthless
μάλιστα (adv.), most of all, abov all
μᾶλλον (adv.), more

ὁράω/ὁρῶ, εἶδον, see
παῖς, παιδός, ὁ, son, child
πατήρ, πατρός, ὁ, father
πείθω, persuade; (perf.) trust (+ dat.)
πέρθω, ἔπερσα, sack
πέρνημι/περνάω, sell
πλέω, ἔπλευσα, sail
πνεῦμα, -ατος, τό, wind, blast
ποδαπός, -ή, -όν, from what country?
πόθεν (adv.), from where
πόλις, πόλιος/πόλεως, ἡ, city, city-state
Ῥαδάμανθυς, ὁ, Rhadamanthys
φιλέω/φιλῶ, love, regard w/ affection
χρῆμα, -ατος, τό, thing; (pl.) goods, property
ψεύδομαι, lie
ψεῦδος, -εος, τό, lie

---

but Silenus is too self-interested for that (S), and the Satyrs immediately follow his lead." (Olson, 47)

270 αὐτὸς ἔχ' "keep (the curse of 268-9) for yourself"
272 τοὺς ξένους δὲ μὴ ἀδίκει addressed to the Cyclops τοὺς ξένους here w/ the connotation of "guests" as well as "strangers"
273 τοῦ Ῥαδαμάνθυος gen. of comparison. He was a son of Zeus and brother of Minos so renowned for his wisdom and justice that he was made a judge in Hades
274 πέποιθα 1st sing. perf. act. indic. < πείθω
275 πόθεν ἐπλεύσατ' cf. Od. 9.252, in which the Cyclops asks Odysseus and his crew: πόθεν πλεῖθ'
277 Ἰθακήσιοι sc. ἐσμεν
    γένος acc. of respect
278 πνεύμασιν θαλασσίοις dat. of means
279 ἐξωσθέντες masc. nom. sing. aor. pass. part. < ἐξωθέω

Κύκλωψ

280 ἦ τῆς κακίστης οἳ μετήλθεθ' ἁρπαγὰς
Ἑλένης Σκαμάνδρου γείτον' Ἰλίου πόλιν;

Ὀδυσσεύς

οὗτοι, πόνον τὸν δεινὸν ἐξηντληκότες.

Κύκλωψ

αἰσχρὸν στράτευμά γ', οἵτινες μιᾶς χάριν
γυναικὸς ἐξεπλεύσατ' ἐς γαῖαν Φρυγῶν.

Ὀδυσσεύς

285 θεοῦ τὸ πρᾶγμα· μηδέν' αἰτιῶ βροτῶν.
ἡμεῖς δέ σ', ὦ θεοῦ ποντίου γενναῖε παῖ,
ἱκετεύομέν τε καὶ ψέγομεν ἐλευθέρως·
μὴ τλῇς πρὸς οἴκους σοὺς ἀφιγμένους φίλους
κτανεῖν βοράν τε δυσσεβῆ θέσθαι γνάθοις·

---

280 ἁρπαγὰς pl. for sing., which occurs w/ abstract nouns
281 Σκαμάνδρου γείτον' in *apposition* to Ἰλίου πόλιν
282 τὸν δεινὸν in *apposition* to πόνον, further clarifying it
ἐξηντληκότες masc. nom. pl. perf. act. part. < ἐξαντλέω
283-4 Surprisingly, it is the brutish Cyclops who bluntly and powerfully calls into question the very weak Greek excuse for the legitimacy of their war against the Trojans
283 οἵτινες "in that you"; "the rel. pl. by sense rather than strict congruence is common enough with ὅστις 'marking character of a person...' " (O'Sullivan and Collard, 166)
285 θεοῦ τὸ πρᾶγμα sc. ἦν; this sounds suspiciously like a rather specious claim in order to exculpate both himself and the Greeks (and it probably is meant to be understood as such), but cf. (the admittedly ambiguous) *Iliad* 1.5: Διὸς δ' ἐτελείετο βουλή ("and the will of Zeus was being brought to completion") and *Iliad* 3.164-5 (Priam speaking to Helen): οὔ τί μοι αἰτίη ἐσσί, θεοί νύ μοι αἴτιοί εἰσιν/ οἵ μοι ἐφώρμησαν πόλεμον πολύδακρυν Ἀχαιῶν ("In my opinion,

αἰσχρός, -ά, -όν, shameful, disgraceful
αἰτιάομαι, blame
ἄναξ, ἄνακτος, ὁ, lord
ἁρπαγή, ἡ, abduction
ἀφικνέομαι, arrive at
βορά, ἡ, food
βροτός, ὁ, mortal man
γείτων, -ονος, ὁ/ἡ, neighbor
γενναῖος, -α, -ον, well-born, noble
γνάθος, ἡ, jaw
γυνή, γυναικός, ἡ, woman
δυσσεβής, -ές, impious, godless
εἷς, μία, ἕν, (gen. ἑνός, μιᾶς, ἑνός), one
ἐκπλέω, ἐξέπλευσα, sail away
ἐλευθέρως (adv.), freely, frankly
ἐξαντλέω/ἐξαντλῶ, endure
ἦ (adv.), Is it perhaps? Can it be?
ἱκετεύω, entreat, beseech, beg
κάκιστος, -η, -ον, most/very wicked, horrible, evil, vile
κτείνω, ἔκτανον, kill
μετέρχομαι, μετῆλθον, go to X (acc.) to seek to avenge Y (acc.)

μηδείς, μηδεμία, μηδέν, not one, not even one, nobody
τίθημι, make X (acc.) Y (acc.); (mid.) make (for oneself)
οἶκος, ὁ, house
ὅστις, ἥτις, ὅ τι, who, which
πόνος, ὁ, toil; trouble, suffering
πόντιος, -α, -ον, of the sea (epithet of Poseidon)
Σκάμανδρος, ὁ, Scamander (river that ran near Troy)
στράτευμα, -ατος, τό, expedition, campaign
τίθημι, put
τλάω, dare, have the cruelty, be hard-hearted
φίλος, ὁ, friend
Φρύξ, Φρυγός, ὁ, Phrygian (an inhabitant of the region around Troy in classical times, and thus often used as a poetic equivalent of 'Trojan')
χάριν (adv./prep. + gen.), for the sake of
ψέγω, blame, censure

---

you are not to blame, but the gods are to blame, who stirred up against me this very tearful war of the Achaeans")

285 αἰτιῶ 2nd sing. pres. mid./pass. (dep.) impera. < αἰτιάομαι

288 Note heavy *assonance* of -ῆς, -ὸς and -ους
τλῇς prohibitive subju.
ἀφιγμένους masc. acc. pl. perf. mid./pass. (dep.) part < ἀφικνέομαι
φίλους a bold claim that Odysseus will soon try to justify

289 θέσθαι aor. mid./pass. (w/ act. sense) inf. < τίθημι

290 οἳ τὸν σόν, ὦναξ, πατέρ' ἔχειν ναῶν ἕδρας
ἐρρυσάμεσθα γῆς ἐν Ἑλλάδος μυχοῖς·
ἱερᾶς τ' ἄθραυστος Ταινάρου μένει λιμὴν
Μαλέας τ' ἄκρας κευθμῶνες ἥ τε Σουνίου
δίας Ἀθάνας σῶς ὑπάργυρος πέτρα
295 Γεραίστιοί τε καταφυγαί· τά θ' Ἑλλάδος
†δύσφρον' ὀνείδη† Φρυξὶν οὐκ ἐδώκαμεν.
ὧν καὶ σὺ κοινοῖ· γῆς γὰρ Ἑλλάδος μυχοὺς
οἰκεῖς ὑπ' Αἴτνῃ, τῇ πυριστάκτῳ πέτρᾳ.

290-1 "A specious claim as no part of Greece was under any threat from Troy" (O'Sullivan and Collard, 167)
290 οἳ its antecedent is φίλους: "(we, your friends) who"
ὦναξ = ὦ ἄναξ
ἔχειν virtually an inf. of purp., i.e., "so as to..."
292 Ταινάρου a promontory at the southern end of Laconia. "According to Pausanias (3.23.2), in the harbour beneath it was a statue of Poseidon, and a nearby cave seems to have been sacred to the god (Paus. 2.2.8; 8.7.2; 8.8.2; 8.10.4.)." (O'Sullivan and Collard, 167)
293-5 For the nom. nouns, sc. μένει/μένουσι
293 Μαλέας see 18
κευθμῶνες i.e., harbors
Σουνίου the southern headland of Attica; it had a temple of Poseidon, ruins of which are famously visible to this day. Nearby were the silver mines of Laurion, "from which Athens derived much of its wealth in the 5th century" (Olson, 49)
δίας Ἀθάνας i.e., belonging to Athens, since Athena was the patron deity of the city-state. Ἀθάνας is the Doric form of Athena's name used in tragedy (Attic = Ἀθηνᾶς)

Ἀθάνα, ἡ, Athena
ἄθραυστος, -ον, undamaged, inviolate
Γεραίστιος, -ον, Geraistian, of Geraistos
γῆ, ἡ, land, country
δίδωμι, ἔδωκα, give, grant; surrender
δῖος, δῖα, δῖον, heavenly, divine
ἕδρα, ἡ, seat, sanctuary, temple
Ἑλλάς, -άδος, ἡ, Greece
ἔχω, have, keep, occupy
ἱερός, -ά, -όν, holy
καταφυγή, ἡ, place of refuge
κευθμών, -ῶνος, ὁ, hollow, recess
κοινόω, make common; (mid.) share in, have a share in (+ gen.)

λιμήν, -ένος, ὁ, harbor
Μαλέα, ἡ, Malea
μένω, remain
μυχός, ὁ, corner, fold, nook; furthest point
ναός, ὁ, temple
οἰκέω, inhabit, dwell in
πέπλος, ὁ, cloak, robe
πέτρα, ἡ, rock (frequently of cliffs, ledges, etc. by the sea)
πυρίστακτος, -ον, fire-streaming, dripping w/ fire
ῥύομαι, ἐρρυσάμην, guard, protect
Σούνιον, ου, τό, Sunium
σῶς, σῶν, safe
Ταίναρος, ἡ, Taenarus
ὑπάργυρος, -ον, containing silver

---

295   Γεραίστιοί τε καταφυγαί i.e., the harbor at Geraistus, "which lay at the southwest tip of the island of Euboea and was the site of another well-known temple of Poseidon" (Olson, 49)
τά θ' Ἑλλάδος "and the possessions of Greece" or, possibly, "and the affairs of Greece"

296   †δύσφρον' ὀνείδη† this phrase has been marked w/ obeli (the "dagger"/"cross" symbol) indicating that the line does not scan and that no editor's emendations have been widely accepted. Kovacs, translating Diggle's conjecture (δύσφορον ὄνειδος, "an intolerable disgrace"), has: "We did not suffer the great disgrace of surrendering Greek possessions to the Trojans."
κοινοῖ 2nd sing. pres. mid./pass. indic. < κοινόω

νόμος δὲ θνητοῖς, εἰ λόγους ἀποστρέφῃ,
300 ἱκέτας δέχεσθαι ποντίους ἐφθαρμένους
ξένιά τε δοῦναι καὶ πέπλους ἐπαρκέσαι·
οὐκ ἀμφὶ βουπόροισι πηχθέντας μέλη
ὀβελοῖσι νηδὺν καὶ γνάθον πλῆσαι σέθεν.
ἅλις δὲ Πριάμου γαῖ᾽ ἐχήρωσ᾽ Ἑλλάδα,
305 πολλῶν νεκρῶν πιοῦσα δοριπετῆ φόνον,
ἀλόχους τ᾽ ἀνάνδρους γραῦς τ᾽ ἄπαιδας ὤλεσεν
πολιούς τε πατέρας. εἰ δὲ τοὺς λελειμμένους
σὺ συμπυρώσας δαῖτ᾽ ἀναλώσεις πικράν,
ποῖ τρέψεταί τις; ἀλλ᾽ ἐμοὶ πιθοῦ, Κύκλωψ·

---

299 νόμος δὲ θνητοῖς sc. ἐστι
λόγους i.e., those made in 290-8
300 ἐφθαρμένους masc. acc. pl. perf. pass. part. < φθείρω
301 δοῦναι aor. act. inf. < δίδωμι
302 The construction shifts, w/ the acc. shipwrecked sailors the subj. of the inf.
πηχθέντας masc. acc. pl. aor. pass. part. < πήγνυμι
μέλη acc. of respect
303 νηδὺν καὶ γνάθον *hysteron proteron*
σέθεν = σου
305 δοριπετῆ φόνον i.e., blood from those killed by the spear
306 ἀνάνδρους, ἄπαιδας the adjs. are proleptic (i.e., used in anticipation of their becoming applicable through the action of the vb): "the land of Priam ruined the wives and old ladies, who are now husbandless and childless"
ἄπαιδας take w/ both γραῦς and πολιούς...πατέρας
πηχθέντας masc. acc. pl. aor. pass. part. < πήγνυμι
307 τοὺς λελειμμένους i.e., the Greek men who survived the Trojan War
λελειμμένους masc. acc. pl. perf. mid./pass. part. < λείπω

ἅλις (adv.), enough (and more than enough)
ἄλοχος, -ου, ἡ, wife
ἀμφί (prep. + dat.), all around, upon
ἀναλίσκω, ἀναλώσω, consume
ἄνανδρος, -ον, husbandless
ἄπαις, -αιδος, childless
ἀποστρέφω, turn away; (mid.) reject
βουπόρος, -ον, ox-piercing; βουπόρος ὀβελός, "spit large enough for roasting a whole ox"
γραῦς, γραός, (acc. pl. γραῦς) ἡ, old woman
δαίς, δαιτός, ἡ, meal, food
δέχομαι, receive hospitably
δοριπετής, -ές, spear-fallen
ἐπαρκέω, supply, furnish
θνητός, ὁ, mortal
ἱκέτης, -ου, ὁ, suppliant
λείπω, leave
λόγος, ὁ, word, reason, argument
μέλος, -εος, τό, limb
νεκρός, ὁ, corpse
νηδύς, -ύος, ἡ, stomach, belly
νόμος, ὁ, law, custom
ξένια, τά, hospitality gifts, guest-gifts (usu. food and drink)
ὀβελός, ὁ, spit
ὄλλυμι, ὤλεσα, ruin, destroy
πατήρ, πατρός, ὁ, father
πείθω, persuade; (mid.) obey, listen to (+ dat.)
πέπλος, ὁ, cloak, robe
πήγνυμι, stick or fix on
πικρός, -ά, -όν, bitter
πίμπλημι, ἔπλησα, fill
πίνω, ἔπιον (aor.), drink
ποῖ (adv.), where? to what place?
πολιός, -ά, -όν, gray/grey, gray/grey-haired
πολύς, πολλή, πολύ, much; (pl.) many
συμπυρόω, burn or roast together
τις, τι, (gen. τινος), (indef. pron.) anyone, anything; someone, something; some, a certain
τρέπω, turn X (acc.); (mid./pass.) turn (oneself)
φθείρω, ruin; (pass.) miserable, have suffered loss from shipwreck
φόνος, ὁ, blood (shed in murder), gore, slaughter
χηρόω, make desolate, bereave

---

309 ποῖ τρέψεταί τις; "i.e., for help or rescue, the point being that the obligation to help strangers is so strong that, if it is not respected, it is hard to imagine what other social conventions might be." (Olson, 50)
πιθοῦ 2nd sing. aor. mid. impera. < πείθω

310   πάρες τὸ μάργον σῆς γνάθου, τὸ δ' εὐσεβὲς
      τῆς δυσσεβείας ἀνθελοῦ· πολλοῖσι γὰρ
      κέρδη πονηρὰ ζημίαν ἠμείψατο.

Σιληνός

      παραινέσαι σοι βούλομαι· τῶν γὰρ κρεῶν
      μηδὲν λίπῃς τοῦδ', ἤν τε τὴν γλῶσσαν δάκῃς,
315   κομψὸς γενήσῃ καὶ λαλίστατος, Κύκλωψ.

Κύκλωψ

      ὁ πλοῦτος, ἀνθρωπίσκε, τοῖς σοφοῖς θεός,
      τὰ δ' ἄλλα κόμποι καὶ λόγων εὐμορφία.
      ἄκρας δ' ἐναλίας αἷς καθίδρυται πατὴρ
      χαίρειν κελεύω· τί τάδε προυστήσω λόγῳ;
320   Ζηνὸς δ' ἐγὼ κεραυνὸν οὐ φρίσσω, ξένε,
      οὐδ' οἶδ' ὅτι Ζεύς ἐστ' ἐμοῦ κρείσσων θεός.

---

310 πάρες 2nd sing. aor. act. impera. < παρίημι
     τὸ μάργον lit., "the greedy/gluttonous thing," i.e., "the greed/gluttony"
311 ἀνθελοῦ 2nd sing. aor. mid. impera. < ἀνθαιρέομαι
312 ἠμείψατο gnomic aor. expressing a general truth; translate as a pres.; κέρδη πονηρὰ is its subj.
314 λίπῃς 2nd sing. aor. act. subju. < λείπω; prohibitive subju.
     τοῦδ' i.e., Odysseus
     ἤν...δάκῃς...γενήσῃ FMV condit.
     ἤν = εἰ ἄν (+ subju.)
     δάκῃς 2nd sing. aor. act. subju. < δάκνω
316 ὁ πλοῦτος...θεός sc. ἐστι
319 χαίρειν κελεύω lit., "I urge ἄκρας δ' ἐναλίας... to rejoice," i.e., "I say goodbye to/to hell w/ ἄκρας δ' ἐναλίας..."
     προυστήσω 2nd sing. aor. mid. (w/ act. force) indic. < προΐστημι

ἄκρα, ἡ, cape, headland
ἀλλός, -ή, -ό, other; τὰ ἄλλα, the rest
ἀμείβω, exchange; (mid.) bring X (acc.) to Y (dat.) (in exchange)
ἀνθαιρέομαι, choose X (acc.) instead of Y (gen.)
ἀνθρωπίσκος, ὁ, dim. of ἄνθρωπος (i.e., little man)
βούλομαι, wish, want (+ inf.)
γίγνομαι, γενήσομαι, become
γλῶσσα, ἡ, tongue
δάκνω, bite
δυσσέβεια, ἡ, impiety
ἐνάλιος, -α, -ον, in or on the sea
εὐμορφία, ἡ, elegance
εὐσεβής, -ές, pious, holy
Ζεύς/Ζῆν, Ζηνός, Ζηνί, Ζῆνα, Zeus
ζημία, ἡ, penalty, punishment
καθιδρύω, make to sit down; (pass.) take one's seat in, have an abode or house
κελεύω, urge
κεραυνός, ὁ, thunderbolt
κέρδος, -εος, τό, gain
κομπέω, boast, be nothing but talk
κομψός, -ή, -όν, clever
κρέας, τό, (pl. κρέα), meat, piece of meat
κρείσσων, -ον, mightier
λαλίστατος, -ον, very talkative
λόγος, ὁ, speech
μάργος, -η, -ον, greedy, gluttonous
ὅτι (conj.), that
παραινέω, offer advice,
παρίημι, let go, give up
πλοῦτος, ὁ, wealth
πονηρός, -ά, όν, wicked, base
προΐστημι, put X (acc.) at the beginning of Y (dat.); put X (acc.) forward as a pretense
σοφός, -ή, -όν, wise
φρίσσω, shudder at (+ acc.)
χαίρω, rejoice, be glad; (inf.) hello, goodbye

---

321 οὐδ' οἶδ' lit., "and I do not know," i.e., "I see no reason to believe" (Olson)
ἐμοῦ gen. of comparison

οὔ μοι μέλει τὸ λοιπόν· ὡς δ' οὔ μοι μέλει
ἄκουσον· ὅταν ἄνωθεν ὄμβρον ἐκχέῃ,
ἐν τῇδε πέτρᾳ στέγν' ἔχων σκηνώματα,
325 ἢ μόσχον ὀπτὸν ἤ τι θήρειον δάκος
δαινύμενος εὖ τέγγων τε γαστέρ' ὕπτιος,
ἐπεκπιὼν γάλακτος ἀμφορέα, πέπλον
κρούω, Διὸς βρονταῖσιν εἰς ἔριν κτυπῶν.
ὅταν δὲ βορέας χιόνα Θρῄκιος χέῃ,
330 δοραῖσι θηρῶν σῶμα περιβαλὼν ἐμὸν
καὶ πῦρ ἀναίθων, χιόνος οὐδέν μοι μέλει.
ἡ γῆ δ' ἀνάγκῃ, κἂν θέλῃ κἂν μὴ θέλῃ,
τίκτουσα ποίαν τἀμὰ πιαίνει βοτά.

---

322 μέλει the subj. is Zeus
323 ἄκουσον 2nd sing. aor. act. impera. < ἀκούω
ὅταν = ὅτε ἄν, "whenever" (+ subju.)
325 θήρειον δάκος an (affected?) circumlocution for θήρ ("wild beast"); recall that the Cyclops did eat lion (248)
326 εὖ τέγγων τε γαστέρ' i.e., drinking plentifully
327 ἐπεκπιών i.e., after (or in addition to) eating the meat in 325-6
γάλακτος ἀμφορέα "amphorae were used in sympotic contexts for wine and water; here is a joke on the barbaric incongruity of using one for milk." (O'Sullivan and Collard)
327-8 πέπλον κρούω according to most scholars, this is a reference to masturbation (part of a *double entendre* in this regard w/ the phrase just above it εὖ τέγγων τε γαστέρ'?)
328 Διὸς βρονταῖσιν εἰς ἔριν κτυπῶν i.e., "making so much noise that the sound rivals Zeus' thunder" (Olson)

ἀκούω, hear
ἀμφορεύς, -έως, ὁ, amphora, storage jar
ἀνάγκῃ (adv.), of necessity
ἀναίθω, light up, kindle
ἄνωθεν (adv.), from above
βορέας, -ου, ὁ, north wind
βοτόν, τό, grazing beast, herd animal
βροντή, ἡ, thunder
γαστήρ, -έρος, ἡ, belly
δαίνυμι, give a banquet or feast; (mid.) dine or feast on
δάκος, -εος, τό, beast
δορά, ἡ, skin, hide
ἐκχέω, pour out
ἐμός, -ή, -όν, my
ἐπεκπίνω, ἐπεξέπιον, drink X (acc.) dry, drain X (acc.) after or in addition to
ἔρις, -ιδος, (acc. ἔριν) ἡ, rivalry; εἰς ἔριν, "in rivalry w/ X (dat.)," "to rival X (dat.)"
εὖ (adv.), well
θέλω, wish
θήρ, θηρός, ὁ, wild beast
θήρειος, -ον, of wild beasts
Θρῄκιος, -α, -ον, Thracian

κρούω, strike, bang
κτυπέω, make X (acc.) resound
λοιπόν (adv., w/ or w/out article τό), in the future, for the future
μέλω, be an object of care or concern to X (dat.)
μόσχος, ὁ/ἡ, calf, young bull
ὄμβρος, ὁ, heavy rain, thunderstorm
ὀπτός, -ή, -όν, roasted
οὐδείς, οὐδεμία, οὐδέν, no one, nobody, nothing
περιβάλλω, περιέβαλον, wrap X (acc.) w/ or in Y (dat.)
πιαίνω, fatten
ποία, ἡ, grass
πῦρ, πυρός, τό, fire
σκήνωμα, -ατος, τό, tent; (mostly in pl.) (military) quarters
στεγνός, -ή, -όν, waterproof
σῶμα, -ατος, τό, body
τέγγω, wet, moisten, soak
τίκτω, bring forth
ὕπτιος, -η, -ον, lying on one's back
χέω, pour
χιών, -όνος, ἡ, snow
ὡς (adv.), how?

---

329 βορέας...Θρῄκιος "Thrace was the extreme northern border of the eastern Mediterranean (where *Cyclops* was written and performed) although not of the western Mediterranean (where Polphemus was supposed to live)." (Olson, 51)

330-1 περιβαλών...ἀναίθων so-called "hanging nominatives," since there is no 1st sing. vb.; the sense, however, despite the *anacoluthon*, is clear

331 οὐδέν μοι μέλει ring-composition w/ οὔ μοι μέλει (322)

332 κἂν θέλῃ κἂν μὴ θέλῃ i.e., whether it wishes to or not κἂν = καὶ ἐάν [= εἰ ἄν], "even if" (+ subju.)

333 τἀμά = τὰ ἐμά

ἀγὼ οὔτινι θύω πλὴν ἐμοί, θεοῖσι δ' οὔ,
335 καὶ τῇ μεγίστῃ, γαστρὶ τῇδε, δαιμόνων.
ὡς τοὐμπιεῖν γε καὶ φαγεῖν τοὐφ' ἡμέραν,
Ζεὺς οὗτος ἀνθρώποισι τοῖσι σώφροσιν,
λυπεῖν δὲ μηδὲν αὐτόν. οἳ δὲ τοὺς νόμους
ἔθεντο ποικίλλοντες ἀνθρώπων βίον,
340 κλαίειν ἄνωγα· τὴν ⟨δ'⟩ ἐμὴν ψυχὴν ἐγὼ
οὐ παύσομαι δρῶν εὖ, κατεσθίων γε σέ.
ξένια δὲ λήψῃ τοιάδ', ὡς ἄμεμπτος ὦ,
πῦρ καὶ πατρῷον τόνδε λέβητά θ', ὃς ζέσας
σὴν σάρκα δυσφάρωτον ἀμφέξει καλῶς.
345 ἀλλ' ἕρπετ' εἴσω, τοῦ κατ' αὔλιον θεοῦ
ἵν' ἀμφὶ βωμὸν στάντες εὐωχῆτέ με.

---

334   ἀγὼ = ἃ ἐγὼ
336-8 τοὐμπιεῖν γε καὶ φαγεῖν...λυπεῖν the article (τοὐμπιεῖν = τὸ ἐμπιεῖν) is shared by all three (articular) infs., thus uniting them as a single concept, i.e., "to drink one's fill and eat...and worry..."
336   τοὐφ' ἡμέραν = τὸ ἐπὶ ἡμέραν, lit. "the thing on the day," i.e., "day by day," "on a daily basis"
337   Ζεὺς οὗτος sc. ἐστι, and cf. 316
      οὗτος should be neut. (i.e., τοῦτο), in agreement w/ τοὐμπιεῖν..., but attracted into the case of its predicate, Ζεὺς
      τοῖσι σώφροσιν in apposition to ἀνθρώποισι, further clarifying it; note the Cyclops' "redefinition of the cardinal Greek virtue of σωφροσύνη (lit., 'sound mindedness', 'moderation', 'self-control'), since he makes gluttony and self-indulgence prescribed behaviour. This is the opposite of what σωφροσύνη normally connoted in Greek usage" (O'Sullivan and Collard)
338   αὐτόν = (Attic contracted form of) ἑαυτόν
339   ἔθεντο 3rd pl. aor. mid. indic. < τίθημι

ἄμεμπτος, -ον, blameless
ἀμπέχω, surround, encase
ἀμφί (prep. + acc.), around
ἄνωγα (perf. w/ pres. sense), command, order, urge
αὔλιον, τό, cave, cavern
βίος, ὁ, life
βωμός, ὁ, altar
δαίμων, -ονος, ὁ/ἡ, god,
διαφόρητος, -ον, torn to pieces, taken apart
δράω, do; + εὖ, do X (acc.) a good turn, treat X (acc.) well
ἑαυτοῦ, -ῆς, -οῦ, himself, herself, itself
εἴσω (adv.), inside
ἐμπίνω, ἐνέπιον, drink one's fill, drink greedily
ἕρπω, go
ἐσθίω, ἔφαγον, eat
εὐωχέω, entertain sumptuously, furnish X (acc.) w/ a feast
ζέω, boil, come to a boil
ἡμέρα, ἡ, day
θύω, sacrifice
ἵνα (conj.), so that, in order that (+ subju. in primary sequence)
ἵστημι, ἔστην, make to stand; (2nd aor. act.) stand

καλῶς (adv.), beautifully, nicely
κατά (prep. + acc.), (down) in
κατεσθίω, eat up, devour
κλαίω, cry, wail
λαμβάνω, λήψομαι, receive
λέβης, -ητος, ὁ, kettle, cauldron
λυπέω, distress, worry
μέγιστος, -η, -ον, greatest
μηδέν (adv.), not at all
νόμος, ὁ, law
ξένια, τά, hospitality gifts, guest-gifts (usu. food and drink)
οὖτις, οὖτι, no one, nothing
πατρῷος, -α, -ον, of my father, hereditary, ancestral
παύω, παύσομαι, stop
πλήν (adv.), except
ποικίλλω, complicate
σάρξ, σαρκός, ἡ, flesh
σώφρων, -ονος, sensible, wise; temperate, self-controlled
τίθημι, set, put; (mid.) make
τοιόσδε, -άδε, -όνδε, such as this, of such a kind
ψυχή, ἡ, spirit
ὡς (adv.), so, thus; (conj.) so that, in order that (+ subju. in primary sequence)

---

340 κλαίειν ἄνωγα i.e., "I tell them to go to hell!"; for the colloquialism, see 174 and note ad loc.

342 ξένια in the following lines (344-5), Polyphemus enumerates the hospitality gifts Odysseus requested in 301 ὦ 1st sing. pres. act. subju. < εἰμί

343 πατρῷον τόνδε λέβητά "a parody of the conventions of heroic gift-giving, which often involes bronze vessels or armor (S) and in which the objects exchanged are frequently given an elaborate pedigree." (Olson, 52). Also note that in the Od., λέβης most often refers to the basin in which the purifying water was handed to the guests before meals

Ὀδυσσεύς

αἰαῖ, πόνους μὲν Τρωϊκοὺς ὑπεξέδυν
θαλασσίους τε, νῦν δ' ἐς ἀνδρὸς ἀνοσίου
ὠμὴν κατέσχον ἀλίμενόν τε καρδίαν.
350   ὦ Παλλάς, ὦ δέσποινα Διογενὲς θεά,
νῦν νῦν ἄρηξον· κρείσσονας γὰρ Ἰλίου
πόνους ἀφῖγμαι κἀπὶ κινδύνου βάθη.
σύ τ', ὦ φαεννὰς ἀστέρων οἰκῶν ἕδρας
Ζεῦ ξένι', ὅρα τάδ'· εἰ γὰρ αὐτὰ μὴ βλέπεις,
355   ἄλλως νομίζῃ, Ζεῦ, τὸ μηδὲν ὢν θεός.

Χορός

Εὐρείας λάρυγγος, ὦ Κύκλωψ,
ἀναστόμου τὸ χεῖλος· ὡς ἕτοιμά σοι
ἑφθὰ καὶ ὀπτὰ καὶ ἀνθρακιᾶς ἄπο ⟨θερμὰ⟩
χναύειν βρύκειν
κρεοκοπεῖν μέλη ξένων
360   δασυμάλλῳ ἐν αἰγίδι κλινομένῳ.

---

350 Παλλάς Athena assisted Odysseus throughout the *Od.*, but conspicuously not in books 9-12, a period which lasted 10 years and included his encounter w/ the Cyclops
351 ἄρηξον sc. μοι
Ἰλίου gen. of comparison; lit., "than Troy," i.e., "than those πόνους I had experienced at Troy"
352 ἀφῖγμαι 1st sing. perf. mid./pass. (dep.) indic. < ἀφικνέομαι
κἀπὶ = καὶ ἐπὶ
353 φαεννὰς ἕδρας an example of *hypallage*, in which a word, instead of agreeing w/ the case it logically qualifies (here ἀστέρων), is made to agree grammatically w/ another case

αἰαῖ (exclamation of horror or surprise), ah!
αἰγίς, -ίδος, ἡ, goatskin
ἀλίμενος, -ον, harborless
ἄλλως (adv.), in vain
ἀναστομόω, open up; (mid.) open X (acc.) of Y (gen.) wide
ἀνήρ, ἀνδρός, ὁ, man
ἀνθρακιά, ἡ, burning charcoal
ἀνόσιος, -ον, godless, unholy
ἀρήγω, help (+ dat.)
ἀστήρ, -έρος, ὁ, star
ἀφικνέομαι, come to
βάθος, -εος, τό, depth
βλέπω, see
βρύκω, eat w/ much noise, eat greedily, gobble
δασύμαλλος, -ον, wooly, thick-fleeced
δέσποινα, ἡ, mistress
Διογενής, -ές, born of Zeus
ἕδρα, ἡ, seat, abode (esp. of the gods)
ἑτοῖμος, -ον, ready
εὐρύς, εὐρεῖα, εὐρύ, wide
ἑφθός, -ή, -όν, boiled
θαλάσσιος, -α, -ον, of, in, on, or from the sea
θεά, ἡ, goddess
θερμός, -ή, -όν, hot
καρδία, ἡ, heart

κατέχω, κατέσχον, hold back; (intrans.) come to shore, land
κίνδυνος, ὁ, danger
κλίνω, make to bend; (pass.) lie down, recline
κρείσσων, -ον, greater
κρεοκοπέω, hack or tear in pieces
λάρυγξ, -υγγος, ὁ, gullet, throat
μέλος, -εος, τό, limb
μηδέν (adv.. w/ or w/out τό), not at all, in no way at all
νομίζω, worship
νῦν (now), now
ξένιος, -α, -ον, belonging to friendship and hospitality; (epithet of Zeus) protector of the rights of hospitality
οἰκέω, inhabit, dwell in
ὀπτός, -ή, -όν, roasted
Παλλάς, -άδος, ἡ, Pallas (epithet of Athena)
πόνος, ὁ, trouble, suffering
Τρωϊκός, -ή, -όν, Trojan
ὑπεκδύομαι, ὑπεξέδυν, escape
φαεινός, -ή, -όν, shining, bright
χεῖλος, -εος, τό, lip
χναύω, gnaw, nibble
ὠμός, -ή, -όν, raw, savage, cruel
ὡς (conj.), as, since

---

355 At the end of Odysseus' speech, Polyphemus drives him and his men into the cave
357 ἀναστόμου 2nd sing. pres. mid. impera. < ἀναστομόω
357-8 ἕτοιμά σοι... sc. ἐστι
358 ἀνθρακιᾶς ἄπο <θερμὰ> cf. 244-5
359 χναύειν βρύκειν κρεοκοπεῖν note *asyndeton*, which imparts a liveliness to the description
360 δασυμάλλῳ this adj. only occurs elsewhere at *Od.* 9.425
κλινομένῳ modifying σοι in 357

μὴ 'μοὶ μὴ προσδίδου·
μόνος μόνῳ γέμιζε πορθμίδος σκάφος.
χαιρέτω μὲν αὖλις ἅδε,
χαιρέτω δὲ θυμάτων
365 ἀποβώμιος ἃν ἀνέχει θυσία
Κύκλωψ Αἰτναῖος ξενικῶν
κρεῶν κεχαρμένος βορᾷ.

370 νηλής, τλᾶμον, ὅστε δωμάτων
371 ἐφεστίους ἱκτῆρας ἐκθύει ξένους,
373 ἑφθά τε δαινύμενος, μυσαροῖσί τ' ὀδοῦσιν
372 κόπτων βρύκων
374 θέρμ' ἀπ' ἀνθράκων κρέα.
<..>

---

361 **μὴ 'μοὶ μὴ** note *alliteration* and repetition, adding emphasis
'μοὶ both a dat. of feeling (aka an ethical dat.: "for my sake," "I beg you") and an indir. obj.
προσδίδου 2nd sing. pres. act. impera. < προσδίδωμι; sc. it/them
362 **μόνῳ** sc. σεαυτῷ; dat. of advantage
πορθμίδος σκάφος i.e., the hollow of your belly
363 **χαιρέτω** 3rd sing. pres. act. impera. < χαίρω; lit., "let αὖλις ἅδε rejoice," i.e., "goodbye and good riddance to αὖλις ἅδε!"
αὖλις i.e., the cave
ἅδε = (Doric form of) ἥδε
364-6 **χαιρέτω...Αἰτναῖος** = δὲ χαιρέτω ἀποβώμιος θυσία θυμάτων ἃν Κύκλωψ Αἰτναῖος ἀνέχει
366 **Αἰτναῖος** see 20
367 **κεχαρμένος** masc. nom. sing. perf. pass. part. < χαίρω

Αἰτναῖος, -α, -ον, of or
  belonging to Aetna, Aetnean
ἀνέχω, hold up (as an offering)
ἄνθραξ, -ακος, ὁ, charcoal
ἀποβώμιος, -ον, godless (lit.
  far from an altar)
αὖλις, -ιδος, ἡ, place for
  passing the night in
βορά, ἡ, meat, food (eaten by
  carnivorous wild animals)
γεμίζω, fill full of, load, or
  freight w/ (a cargo of a ship)
δαίνυμι, give a banquet or feast;
  (mid.) dine or feast on
δῶμα, -ατος, τό, house (pl.
  often = sing., esp. in verse)
ἐκθύω, sacrifice
ἐφέστιος, -ον, at one's own
  fireside, (of suppliants who
  claim protection by) sitting by
  the fireside
θῦμα, -ατος, τό, victim

θυσία, ἡ, sacrifice
ἱκτήρ, -ῆρος, ὁ, suppliant
κόπτω, tear, cut up into pieces
κρέας, τό, (pl. κρέα), flesh,
  piece of flesh or meat
μόνος, -η, -ον, alone
μυσαρός, -ά, -όν, loathsome;
  polluted
νηλής, ές, pitiless
ξενικός, -ή, -όν, of a stranger or
  guest
ὀδούς, -όντος, ὁ, tooth
ὅστε, ἥτε, ὅτε, who, which
πορθμίς, -ίδος, ἡ, ship
προσδίδωμι, give a share of,
  give some
σκάφος, -εος, τό, hull (of a ship)
τλήμων, -ονος, reckless,
  shameless
χαίρω, rejoice; take pleasure in
  (+ dat.) (pass. w/ same sense as
  act.)

---

370 τλᾶμον = (Doric form of) τλῆμον (masc. voc. sing.)
    νηλής...ὅστε sc. ἐστι; νηλής is the adj. Odysseus uses to
    describe the Cyclops at *Od.* 9.287
373-2 "The lines are transposed in order to restore metrical
    corresponsion with 358, and with it the identical placing of
    the words βρύκειν in 358 and βρύκων in 372." (O'Sullivan
    and Collard, 178)
373 μυσαροῖσί τ' ὀδοῦσιν dat. of means
372 κόπτων βρύκων asyndeton (cf. 358-9 and note ad loc.)
374 A lacuna is posited by most editors after this line since an
    entire verse is needed to complete response w/ the strophe

Ὀδυσσεύς

375 ὦ Ζεῦ, τί λέξω, δείν' ἰδὼν ἄντρων ἔσω
κοὐ πιστά, μύθοις εἰκότ' οὐδ' ἔργοις βροτῶν;

Χορός

τί δ' ἔστ', Ὀδυσσεῦ; μῶν τεθοίναται σέθεν
φίλους ἑταίρους ἀνοσιώτατος Κύκλωψ;

Ὀδυσσεύς

δισσούς γ' ἀθρήσας κἀπιβαστάσας χεροῖν,
380 οἳ σαρκὸς εἶχον εὐτραφέστατον πάχος.

Χορός

πῶς, ὦ ταλαίπωρ', ἦτε πάσχοντες τάδε;

Ὀδυσσεύς

ἐπεὶ πετραίαν τήνδ' ἐσήλθομεν στέγην,
ἀνέκαυσε μὲν πῦρ πρῶτον, ὑψηλῆς δρυὸς
κορμοὺς πλατείας ἐσχάρας βαλὼν ἔπι,
385 τρισσῶν ἁμαξῶν ὡς ἀγώγιμον βάρος,
καὶ χάλκεον λέβητ' ἐπέζεσεν πυρί,

375-6 Unlike in the *Od.*, where Odysseus is trapped inside the Cyclops' cave by a giant rock that the monster has put over the entrance, here he "reappears and recounts in the manner of a messenger in a tragedy events too violent and tumultuous to be depicted before the audience." (O'Sullivan and Collard, 178)

375 λέξω 1st sing. aor. act. subju.; deliberative subju.

376 κοὐ = καὶ οὐ
μύθοις εἰκότ' Odysseus' realization that he is a character in a "myth" is a unique "meta" comment of the kind never found in fifth-century tragedy (and only rarely in comedy) εἰκότ' neut. acc. pl. perf. act. part. < ἔοικα

ἀγώγιμος, -ον, capable of being carried; w/ βάρος, enough to load (+ gen.)
ἀθρέω, look at, observe, perceive
ἄμαξα, ἡ, wagon
ἀνακαίω, ἀνέκαυσα, kindle
ἀνοσιώτατος, -ον, most unholy or godless
βάρος, -ους, τό, weight, load
βροτός, ὁ, mortal man
δεινός, -ή, -όν, terrible
δισσός, -ή, -όν, double; (pl.) two
δρῦς, δρυός, ἡ, oak (tree)
εἰσέρχομαι, εἰσῆλθον, enter
ἔοικα (perf. w/ pres. sense), be like; (part.) like
ἐπεί (conj.), when
ἐπιβαστάζω, weigh in the hand
ἐπιζέω, heat X (acc.) over Y (dat.)
ἔργον, τό, deed
ἐσχάρα, ἡ, hearth
ἔσω/εἴσω (adv.; prep. + gen.), inside, within
ἑταῖρος, ὁ, comrade, companion

εὐτραφέστατος, -η, -ον, most well-fed, fattest
θοινάω (mid./pass. = act.), feast on
κορμός, ὁ, trunk, log
λέβης, -ητος, ὁ, cauldron
μῦθος, ὁ, story, tale, myth
πάσχω, endure
πάχος, -εος, τό, thickness
πετραῖος, -α, -ον, rocky
πιστός, -ή, -όν, to be believed
πλατύς, -εῖα, -ύ, broad, wide
πρῶτον (adv.), first
πῶς (adv.), how? in what manner?
σάρξ, σαρκός, ἡ, flesh
στέγη, ἡ, chamber, room
ταλαίπωρος, -ον, suffering, miserable
τρισσός, -ή, -όν, threefold; (pl.) three
ὑψηλός, -ή, -όν, high, lofty
φίλος, -η, -ον, dear
χάλκεος, -έα, -εον, bronze
χείρ, χειρός, ἡ, hand
ὡς (adv.), about, approximately

---

377 μῶν = μὴ οὖν, "It can't be, can it?"
τεθοίναται 3rd sing. perf. mid./pass. indic. < θοινάω
σέθεν = σου

379 γ' "(yes), in fact, (he did eat them)"
χεροῖν dat. dual; dat. of means

381 "The point of the question is not that the chorus are astonished at what has gone on...but that they want a more detailed account of the events described briefly in 379f..." (Olson, 55)
ἦτε πάσχοντες periphrastic construction (form of εἰμί [here imperf.] + pres. part.) in place of imperf. indic. (ἐπάσχετε)

384 πλατείας ἐσχάρας...ἔπι = ἔπι πλατείας ἐσχάρας

ἔπειτα φύλλων ἐλατίνων χαμαιπετῆ
ἔστρωσεν εὐνὴν πλησίον πυρὸς φλογί.
κρατῆρα δ' ἐξέπλησεν ὡς δεκάμφορον,
μόσχους ἀμέλξας, λευκὸν ἐσχέας γάλα,
390 σκύφος τε κισσοῦ παρέθετ' εἰς εὖρος τριῶν
πήχεων, βάθος δὲ τεσσάρων ἐφαίνετο,
ὀβελούς τ', ἄκρους μὲν ἐγκεκαυμένους πυρί,
ξεστοὺς δὲ δρεπάνῳ τἄλλα, παλιούρου κλάδων,
395 †Αἰτναῖά τε σφαγεῖα πελέκεων γνάθοις†.
ὡς δ' ἦν ἕτοιμα πάντα τῷ θεοστυγεῖ
Ἅιδου μαγείρῳ, φῶτε συμμάρψας δύο
ἔσφαζ' ἑταίρων τῶν ἐμῶν, ῥυθμῷ θ' ἑνὶ,
τὸν μὲν λέβητος ἐς κύτος χαλκήλατον

---

389 ἐσχέας masc. nom. sing. aor. act. part. < ἐσχέω/εἰσχέω
390 σκύφος τε κισσοῦ cf. *Od.* 9.346, where Odysseus gives Polyphemus wine to drink poured out of a κισσύβιον, a rustic drinking cup (so called either as made of ivy-wood or adorned w/ painted or carved ivy-wreaths)
παρέθετ' 3rd sing. aor. mid. indic. < παρατίθημι
391 πήχεων a cubit is the distance from one's elbow to the tip of one's extended finger (i.e., about 18 inches/46 cm)
393 ἐγκεκαυμένους masc. acc. pl. perf. mid./pass. part. < ἐγκαίω
394 δρεπάνῳ dat. of means
τἄλλα = τὰ ἄλλα, acc. pl., here an acc. of respect (i.e., w/ adv. force), "with respect to the rest (of the spits)," "as for the rest (of the spits)"
394 παλιούρου κλάδων both explains why the branches needed to be smoothed and indicates that the Cyclops is operating on a level more primitive than his human victims, who employed metal spits

Ἅιδης, -ου, ὁ, Hades
ἄκρος, -α, -ον, farthest point or end
ἀλλός, -ή, -ό, other; τὰ ἄλλα, the rest
ἀμέλγω, milk
βάθος, -εος, τό, depth, height
γάλα, γάλακτος, τό, milk
δεκάμφορος, -ον, holding 10 amphoras (i.e., c. 90 gallons/341 liters)
δρέπανον, τό, scythe
δύο (indecl.), two
ἐγκαίω, burn in (+ dat.)
εἰς (prep. + acc.), as far as
εἷς, μία, ἕν, (gen. ἑνός, μιᾶς, ἑνός), one
ἐκπίμπλημι, ἐξέπλησα, fill up
ἐλάτινος, η, ον, of the fir tree
ἔπειτα (adv.), then
ἐσχέω/εἰσχέω, pour in
ἑτοῖμος, -ον, ready
εὐνή, ἡ, bed
εὖρος, εος, τό, breadth, width; w/ εἰς, in breadth or width
θεοστυγής, -ές, loathed by the gods, vile
κισσός, ὁ, ivy (wood)
κλάδος, ὁ, branch
κρατήρ, -ῆρος, ὁ, mixing bowl (usu. used for mixing wine and water)
κύτος, -εος, τό, hollow
λευκός, -ή, -όν, white
μάγειρος, ὁ, butcher
μόσχος, ὁ/ἡ, calf, young bull
ξεστός, -ή, -όν, smoothed
ὀβελός, ὁ, spit
παλίουρος, ὁ, thorn bush
παρατίθημι, place X (acc.) next to; (mid.) place or set X (acc.) before oneself
πᾶς, πᾶσα, πᾶν, all, every
πῆχυς, πήχεος, ὁ, cubit
πλησίον (adv./prep. + dat.), near to
ῥυθμός, ὁ, movement
σκύφος, -εος, τό, cup
στρώννυμι, ἔστρωσα, spread out
συμμάρπτω, seize or grasp together
σφάζω, cut the throat of
τέσσαρες, τέσσαρα, four
φαίνω, bring to light; (pass.) be seen (to be), appear (to be)
φλόξ, φλογός, ἡ, flame
φύλλον, τό, leaf; (pl.) foliage
φώς, φωτός, ὁ, man
χαλκήλατος, -ον, of beaten brass or bronze
χαμαιπετής, -ές, lying on the ground
ὡς (+ past tense indic. vb.) when

---

395 A seemingly corrupt line; for details, see O'Sullivan and Collard (180-1). As printed, the line lit. = "and Aetnean sacrificial bowls, with (or for) the jaws of (his?) axes"
397 φῶτε acc. dual (tautologous w/ δύο)
συμμάρψας the same vb. (in *tmesis*) is used in *Od*. 9.289 describing the same action: σὺν δὲ δύω μάρψας
398 ῥυθμῷ θ' ἐνὶ dat. of means
399-400 τὸν μὲν... τὸν δ' αὖ "one man...the other in turn..."

⟨..................................⟩

400 τὸν δ' αὖ, τένοντος ἁρπάσας ἄκρου ποδός,
παίων πρὸς ὀξὺν στόνυχα πετραίου λίθου
ἐγκέφαλον ἐξέρρανε· καὶ διαρταμῶν
λάβρῳ μαχαίρᾳ σάρκας ἐξῶπτα πυρί,
τὰ δ' ἐς λέβητ' ἐφῆκεν ἕψεσθαι μέλη.
405 ἐγὼ δ' ὁ τλήμων δάκρυ' ἀπ' ὀφθαλμῶν χέων
ἐχριμπτόμην Κύκλωπι κἀδιακόνουν·
ἄλλοι δ' ὅπως ὄρνιθες ἐν μυχοῖς πέτρας
πτήξαντες εἶχον, αἷμα δ' οὐκ ἐνῆν χροΐ.
ἐπεὶ δ' ἑταίρων τῶν ἐμῶν πλησθεὶς βορᾶς
410 ἀνέπεσε, φάρυγος αἰθέρ' ἐξανεὶς βαρύν,
ἐσῆλθέ μοί τι θεῖον· ἐμπλήσας σκύφος
Μάρωνος αὐτῷ τοῦδε προσφέρω πιεῖν,

---

399 After 399, it seems a verse (or two), containing a vb. such as ἔβαλε ("threw") or ἔρριψε ("hurled") has dropped out
401-2 παίων...ἐξέρρανε the actions and vocabulary are similar to that of *Od.* 9.289-90
403 λάβρῳ μαχαίρᾳ...πυρί dat. of means x2
404 ἕψεσθαι epexegetical (i.e., explanatory) inf. (more common in verse than in prose); so too πιεῖν in 412
406 κἀδιακόνουν = καὶ ἐδιακόνουν; often remarked upon by commentators as an "odd detail, since by Odysseus' own admission he has not yet hit on his great plan (cf. 409-11) and thus has no need to try to win the monster's confidence." (Olson, 56)
407-8 ἐν μυχοῖς πέτρας πτήξαντες εἶχον the details are similar to *Od.* 9.236
408 πτήξαντες εἶχον periphrastic construction, stressing the permanence of the result; i.e., "remained crouching"

αἰθήρ, -έρος, ἡ, air
αἷμα, -ατος, τό, blood
ἀναπίπτω, ἀνέπεσον, lay back
ἁρπάζω, seize quickly, snatch up (by + gen.)
βαρύς, -εῖα, -ύ, strong, disgusting
βορά, ἡ, meat, food (eaten by carnivorous wild animals)
δάκρυον, τό, tear
διακονέω, be servant to, attend on (+ dat.)
διαρταμέω, cut limb from limb
ἐγκέφαλος, ὁ, brain(s)
ἐκραίνω, ἐξέρρανον, cause to splatter out
ἐμπίμπλημι, ἐνέπλησα, fill X (acc.) with Y (gen.)
ἔνειμι, be in
ἐξανίημι, send forth, let loose
ἐξοπτάω, roast thoroughly
ἐφίημι, ἐφῆκα, throw
ἔχω, have, hold, keep
ἕψω, boil
θεῖος, -α, -ον, of, from, or sent by a god, divine
λάβρος, -ον, violent, fierce
λίθος, ὁ, stone

Μάρων, -ωνος, ὁ, Maron
μάχαιρα, ἡ, large knife (used for carving meat)
μέλος, -εος, τό, limb
μυχός, ὁ, corner, nook, recess
ὀξύς, -εῖα, -ύ, sharp
ὅπως (conj.), as, like
ὄρνις, ὄρνιθος, ὁ, bird
ὀφθαλμός, ὁ, eye
παίω, strike
πέτρα, ἡ, rock (frequently of cliffs, ledges, etc. by the sea)
πίμπλημι, fill with (+ gen.)
πίνω, ἔπιον (aor.), drink
πούς, ποδός, ὁ, foot
προσφέρω, present, offer, give
πτήσσω, ἔπτηξα, crouch or cower down in fear
στόνυξ, -υχος, ὁ, point
τένων, -οντος, ὁ, tendon
τλήμων, -ονος, ὁ/ἡ, suffering, wretched, miserable
φάρυγξ, φάρυγ(γ)ος, ὁ, throat, gullet
χέω, pour
χρίμπτω, bring near; (pass.) draw near to, approach (+ dat.)
χρώς, χροός, ὁ, skin, complexion

---

409 πλησθεὶς masc. nom. sing. aor. pass. part. < πίμπλημι
410 φάρυγος'...βαρύν i.e., after belching loudly. Note that αἰθέρ'...βαρύν is "a virtual oxymoron as αἰθήρ typically denotes the upper air, the air of heaven as something bright and pure..., but it can mean any air or vapour as at 629; and βαρύς here denotes something from the depths that is disgusting or noisome." (O'Sullivan and Collard, 182)
ἐξανεὶς masc. nom. sing. aor. act. part. < ἐξανίημι
411 τι θεῖον i.e., a brilliant idea; contrast this w/ *Od.* 9.318
412 Μάρωνος *metonomy* (or ellipse) for Maron's wine, which had been given to Odysseus by Maron (*Od.* 9.196-211)
τοῦδε partitive gen., i.e., "some of this (wine)"

λέγων τάδ'· Ὦ παῖ ποντίου θεοῦ Κύκλωψ,
σκέψαι τόδ' οἷον Ἑλλὰς ἀμπέλων ἄπο
415 θεῖον κομίζει πῶμα, Διονύσου γάνος.
ὁ δ' ἔκπλεως ὢν τῆς ἀναισχύντου βορᾶς
ἐδέξατ' ἔσπασέν ⟨τ'⟩ ἄμυστιν ἑλκύσας
κἀπῄνεσ' ἄρας χεῖρα· Φίλτατε ξένων,
καλὸν τὸ πῶμα δαιτὶ πρὸς καλῇ δίδως.
420 ἡσθέντα δ' αὐτὸν ὡς ἐπῃσθόμην ἐγώ,
ἄλλην ἔδωκα κύλικα, γιγνώσκων ὅτι
τρώσει νιν οἶνος καὶ δίκην δώσει τάχα.
καὶ δὴ πρὸς ᾠδὰς εἷρπ'. ἐγὼ δ' ἐπεγχέων
ἄλλην ἐπ' ἄλλῃ σπλάγχν' ἐθέρμαινον ποτῷ.
425 ᾄδει δὲ παρὰ κλαίουσι συνναύταις ἐμοῖς
ἄμουσ', ἐπηχεῖ δ' ἄντρον. ἐξελθὼν δ' ἐγὼ
σιγῇ σὲ σῶσαι κἄμ', ἐὰν βούλῃ, θέλω.

---

414 σκέψαι 2nd sing. aor. mid./pass. impera. < σκέπτομαι
417 ἔσπασέν ⟨τ'⟩ ἄμυστιν ἑλκύσας all three words are synonyms, emphasizing the crude, barbaric nature of the Cyclops. ἄμυστιν is an internal acc.
418 κἀπῄνεσ' = καὶ ἐπῄνεσ'; sc. it
ἄρας χεῖρα either the gesture signals the Cyclops' admiration or he is signaling for another drink (or both)
420 ἡσθέντα masc. acc. sing. aor. pass. (dep.) part. < ἥδομαι
422 νιν = (Doric form of) αὐτόν/αὐτήν
423 καὶ δή "and then straightaway" (Olson), "sure enough" (O'Sullivan and Collard)
πρὸς ᾠδὰς εἷρπ' i.e., he started singing
εἷρπ' inchoative imperf.; lit., "he began to move"
424 ἄλλην ἐπ' ἄλλῃ = ἄλλην κύλικα ἐπ' ἄλλῃ, i.e., one cup after another
ποτῷ dat. of means

ἀείδω/ᾄδω, sing
αἴρω, ἦρον, raise, lift up
ἄμουσος, -ον, unmusical, discordant
ἄμπελος, ἡ, grape-vine
ἄμυστις, -ιος, ἡ, deep drinking w/out drawing a breath, chugging
ἀναίσχυντος, -ον, abominable, execrable
βούλομαι, wish
γάνος, -εος, τό, brightness; joy
γιγνώσκω, know, think
δαίς, δαιτός, ἡ, meal, food
δέχομαι, ἐδεξάμην, take
δίδωμι, ἔδωκα, δώσω, give
δίκη, ἡ, justice; penalty; δίδωμι δίκην, "pay a penalty," "suffer punishment"
ἔκπλεως, -ων, quite full of (+ gen.)
ἕλκω, guzzle, chug
Ἑλλάς, -άδος, ἡ, Greece
ἐξέρχομαι, ἐξῆλθον, come out
ἐπαινέω, praise
ἐπαισθάνομαι, ἐπῃσθόμην, perceive
ἐπεγχέω, pour in (upon or after)
ἐπηχέω, echo, resound
ἕρπω, εἷρπον (imperf.), move
θέλω, be willing, intend (+ inf.)
θερμαίνω, warm
ἥδομαι, enjoy oneself, take pleasure

καλός, -ή, -όν, fine
κλαίω, weep, cry, wail
κομίζω, provide
κύλιξ, -ικος, ἡ, cup, wine-cup
λέγω, say
οἶνος, ὁ, wine
οἶος, οἴη, οἶον, what sort, what kind
ὅτι (conj.), that
παρά (prep. + dat.), beside
πόντιος, -α, -ον, of the sea (epithet of Poseidon)
πότος, ὁ, drink, drinking
πρός (prep. + dat.), on top of, in addition to
πῶμα, -ατος, τό, drink
σιγῇ (adv.), in silence, secretly
σκέπτομαι, behold, consider
σπάω, gulp down, drain
σπλάγχνα, τά, innards, guts; heart
συνναύτης, -ου, ὁ, shipmate
σώζω, save, rescue
τάχα (adv.), soon
τιτρώσκω, τρώσω, wound; be one's undoing (Kovacs) or ruin (O'Sullivan and Collard)
φίλτατος, -η, -ον, one's nearest and dearest
χείρ, χειρός, ἡ, hand
ᾠδή, ἡ, song
ὡς (+ past tense indic. vb.) when

427-8 σὲ...βούλῃ...εἴπατ'...χρῄζετ' the chorus is often referred to by other characters in both the sing. and pl.; sometimes the shift between the two is quite abrupt

426-7 ἐξελθών...ἐὰν βούλῃ, θέλω Present General condit.

427 κἄμ' = καὶ ἐμέ
ἐάν = εἰ ἄν (+ subju.)

ἀλλ' εἴπατ' εἴτε χρῄζετ' εἴτ' οὐ χρῄζετε
φεύγειν ἄμεικτον ἄνδρα καὶ τὰ Βακχίου
430 ναίειν μέλαθρα Ναΐδων νυμφῶν μέτα.
ὁ μὲν γὰρ ἔνδον σὸς πατὴρ τάδ' ᾔνεσεν·
ἀλλ' ἀσθενὴς γὰρ κἀποκερδαίνων ποτοῦ
ὥσπερ πρὸς ἰξῷ τῇ κύλικι λελημμένος
πτέρυγας ἀλύει· σὺ δέ (νεανίας γὰρ εἶ)
435 σώθητι μετ' ἐμοῦ καὶ τὸν ἀρχαῖον φίλον
Διόνυσον ἀνάλαβ', οὐ Κύκλωπι προσφερῆ.

Χορός

ὦ φίλτατ', εἰ γὰρ τήνδ' ἴδοιμεν ἡμέραν
Κύκλωπος ἐκφυγόντες ἀνόσιον κάρα.
ὡς διὰ μακροῦ γε †τὸν σίφωνα τὸν φίλον
440 χηρεύομεν τόνδ' οὐκ ἔχομεν καταφαγεῖν.†

---

428 εἴπατ' 2nd pl. aor. act. impera. < εἶπον
432 κἀποκερδαίνων = καὶ ἀποκερδαίνων
433-4 ὥσπερ...ἀλύει "This rather elliptically expressed idea is that Silenus in his drunkenness flails his arms about in the same way as a bird caught by its feet in lime flaps its wings about – either uncontrollably or without achieving anything; but 'bird' does not appear in the simile, its presence being left to inference from 'lime' and 'wings'." (O'Sullivan and Collard, 185)
ἰξῷ a sticky substance prepared from mistletoe berries used to trap birds
τῇ κύλικι dat. of means
λελημμένος masc. nom. sing. perf. mid./pass. part. < λαμβάνω
434 πτέρυγας acc. of respect
435 σώθητι 2nd sing. aor. pass. impera. < σῴζω
437 εἰ γάρ "if only..." (+ opt. of wish)

αἰνέω, praise, assent to, approve
ἀλύω, be excited; struggle
ἄμεικτος, -ον, incapable of mixing w/ others, savage
ἀναλαμβάνω, ἀνέλαβον, get back, regain, recover
ἀνήρ, ἀνδρός, ὁ, man
ἀνόσιος, -ον, godless, impious
ἀποκερδαίνω, derive benefit or enjoyment from X (gen.)
ἀρχαῖος, -α, -ον, old
ἀσθενής, -ές, weak
Βάκχιος/Βάκχος, ὁ, Bacchus (common name/epithet of Dionysus)
εἶπον (aor.; pres. = φημί, λέγω, ἀγορεύω) said
εἴτε...εἴτε (adv.), whether...or
ἐκφεύγω, ἐξέφυγον, escape
ἔνδον (adv.), inside, within
ἡμέρα, ἡ, day
ἰξός, ὁ, bird-lime
κάρα, κάρητος, τό, head

λαμβάνω, catch, seize
μακρός, -ά, -όν, long
μέλαθρον, -ου, τό, main beam which supports the ceiling, roof; (mostly in pl. =) house, hall(s)
μετά (prep. + gen.), with
Ναῖς, Ναΐδος, ἡ, Naiad, a type of nymph associated w/ water and rivers
ναίω, dwell in, inhabit
νεανίας, -ου, ὁ, young
νύμφη, ἡ, nymph
πατήρ, πατρός, ὁ, father
πρός (prep. + dat.), on; against
προσφερής, -ές, similar to, like (+ dat.)
πτέρυξ, -υγος, ἡ, wing
σός, -ή, -όν, your
φεύγω, flee (from), escape
φίλος, ὁ, friend
χρῄζω, desire (+ inf.)
ὡς (conj.), since
ὥσπερ (adv.), just as, like

---

437 ἴδοιμεν 1st pl. aor. act. opt. < ὁράω/ὁρῶ/εἶδον
438 Κύκλωπος...ἀνόσιον κάρα in Attic poets, κάρα is used in a periphrastic sense w/ the gen. of the person's name to refer (usu. honorifically) to their person; i.e., "the godless presence/person of the Cyclops" or even simply "the godless Cyclops"
439 διὰ μακροῦ sc. χρόνου, "for a long time"
439-40 †τὸν σίφωνα... καταφαγεῖν.† lit., "we are widowers w/ respect to this beloved tube/pipe here [and] we don't have [anything] to eat." For the metrical and textual problems, see Seaford 186-7 and O'Sullivan and Collard 185-6. The first phrase refers via a metaphor (tube/pipe = penis) to the satyrs' involuntary sexual abstinence since becoming slaves of the Cyclops

Ὀδυσσεύς

ἄκουε δή νυν ἣν ἔχω τιμωρίαν
θηρὸς πανούργου σῆς τε δουλείας φυγήν.

Χορός

λέγ', ὡς Ἀσιάδος οὐκ ἂν ἥδιον ψόφον
κιθάρας κλύοιμεν ἢ Κύκλωπ' ὀλωλότα.

Ὀδυσσεύς

445 ἐπὶ κῶμον ἕρπειν πρὸς κασιγνήτους θέλει
Κύκλωπας ἡσθεὶς τῷδε Βακχίου ποτῷ.

Χορός

ξυνῆκ'· ἔρημον ξυλλαβὼν δρυμοῖσί νιν
σφάξαι μενοινᾷς ἢ πετρῶν ὦσαι κάτα.

Ὀδυσσεύς

οὐδὲν τοιοῦτον· δόλιος ἡ προθυμία.

Χορός

450 πῶς δαί; σοφόν τοί σ' ὄντ' ἀκούομεν πάλαι.

---

441 ἔχω "I have (in mind)"
443-4 Ἀσιάδος...κλύοιμεν ἢ = οὐκ ἂν κλύοιμεν ψόφον κιθάρας Ἀσιάδος ἥδιον ἢ (κλύοιμεν)...
Ἀσιάδος...κιθάρας ψόφον in many cults of Dionysus, the god was believed to have arrived in Greece from the east as an Asiatic foreigner, and was closely associated with the music of Asia Minor and its religious traditions (esp. that of Cybele, a Phrygian/Anatolian mother goddess) κλύοιμεν potential opt.
444 ὀλωλότα masc. acc. sing. perf. act. part. < ὄλλυμι
446 ἡσθεὶς masc. nom. sing. aor. pass. (dep.) part. < ἥδομαι
447 ξυνῆκ' so-called "dramatic aor.", which is translated as a pres. This use occurs only w/ 1st sing. in the dialogue parts of tragedy and comedy to denote a state of mind occurring to the speaker in the moment just passed

ἀκούω, listen to
Ἀσιάς, -άδος, ἡ, Asia
δαί (colloquial particle), exactly
δόλιος, -α, -ον, deceitful, cunning
δουλεία, ἡ, slavery
δρυμός, ὁ, thicket
ἐρῆμος, -ον, alone, helpless
ἕρπω, go
ἤ (conj.), than; or
ἥδιον (adv.), w/ more pleasure
ἥδομαι, take delight in (+ dat.)
θέλω, want (+ inf.)
θήρ, θηρός, ὁ, wild beast
κασίγνητος, ὁ, brother
κλύω, listen to, hear
κῶμος, ὁ, band of drunken revelers, revel
μενοινάω/μενοινῶ, be eager (+ inf.)
νιν (Doric and Tragic acc. 3rd sing. pron. = αὐτόν, αὐτήν)
νυν (adv.), then
ξυνίημι, ξυνῆκα, understand
ξυλλαμβάνω, ξυνέλαβον, lay hold of, catch
ὄλλυμι, destroy; (perf. act. w/ mid. sense) perish, be destroyed
οὐδείς, οὐδεμία, οὐδέν, no one, nobody, nothing
πάλαι (adv.), long, for a long time
πάνουργος, -ον, ruthless, treacherous
προθυμία, ἡ, purpose, intention
πῶς (adv.), how?
σοφός, -ή, -όν, clever
σφάζω, cut the throat of
τιμωρία, ἡ, vengeance on X (gen.), revenge for X (gen.)
τοι (particle), truly, in truth, surely
τοιοῦτος, -αύτη, -οῦτον, such as this
φυγή, ἡ, flight or escape from (+ gen.)
ψόφος, ὁ, sound
ὠθέω, ἔωσα, push
ὡς (conj.), since

---

447 δρυμοῖσί dat. of place (used in verse); i.e., "in the thickets"

449 οὐδὲν τοιοῦτον sc. μενοινάω/μενοινῶ
δόλιος ἡ προθυμία sc. ἐστι

Ὀδυσσεύς

κώμου μὲν αὐτὸν τοῦδ' ἀπαλλάξαι, λέγων
ὡς οὐ Κύκλωψι πῶμα χρὴ δοῦναι τόδε,
μόνον δ' ἔχοντα βίοτον ἡδέως ἄγειν.
ὅταν δ' ὑπνώσσῃ Βακχίου νικώμενος,
455 ἀκρεμὼν ἐλαίας ἔστιν ἐν δόμοισί τις,
ὃν φασγάνῳ τῷδ' ἐξαποξύνας ἄκρον
ἐς πῦρ καθήσω· κᾆθ' ὅταν κεκαυμένον
ἴδω νιν, ἄρας θερμὸν ἐς μέσην βαλῶ
Κύκλωπος ὄψιν ὄμμα τ' ἐκτήξω πυρί.
460 ναυπηγίαν δ' ὡσεί τις ἁρμόζων ἀνὴρ
διπλοῖν χαλινοῖν τρύπανον κωπηλατεῖ,
οὕτω κυκλώσω δαλὸν ἐν φαεσφόρῳ
Κύκλωπος ὄψει καὶ συναυανῶ κόρας.

---

451 ἀπαλλάξαι sc. μενοινάω/μενοινῶ
452 δοῦναι aor. act. inf. < δίδωμι
453 ἔχοντα sc. πῶμα
454 The details of Odysseus' plan are largely copied from the ones in *Od.* 9.319-28, 375-90
ὅταν = ὅτε ἄν, "whenever" (+ subju.)
Βακχίου = ὑπὸ Βακχίου; vbs. expressing inferiority are freq. followed by the gen.
456 φασγάνῳ τῷδ' dat. of means
ἄκρον acc. of respect
457 κᾆθ' = καὶ εἶτα
κεκαυμένον masc. acc. sing. perf. mid./pass. part. < καίω
459 πυρί dat. of means
461 διπλοῖν χαλινοῖν dat. dual; dat. of means

ἄγω, lead; + βίοτον, "spend or live one's life"
αἴρω, ἦρον, raise, lift up
ἀκρέμων, -όνος, ὁ, branch
ἄκρον, -ον, τό, end, tip
ἀπαλλάσσω, remove, free X (acc.) from Y (gen.)
ἁρμόζω, join together
βάλλω, βαλῶ, throw, thrust, strike
Βάκχιος/Βάκχος, ὁ, Bacchus (common name/epithet of Dionysus)
βίοτος, ὁ, life
δαλός, ὁ, fire-brand, piece of blazing wood
διπλόος, -η, -ον (contracted form διπλοῦς, -ῆ, -οῦν), double, two, pair of
δόμος, ὁ, house (pl. often = sing., esp. in verse)
εἶτα (adv.), then
ἐκτήκω, melt (completely), destroy
ἐλαία, ἡ, olive tree
ἐξαποξύνω, sharpen well
ἡδέως (adv.), pleasantly, w/ pleasure
θερμός, -ή, -όν, hot
καθίημι, καθήσω, put, place
καίω, set on fire, burn

κόρη, ἡ, pupil
κυκλόω, move in a circle, whirl around
κωπηλατέω, move back and forth
μέσος, -η, -ον, the middle of
μόνος, -η, -ον, alone, solitary, w/out others
ναυπηγία, ἡ, shipbuilding, material for building a ship, wood
νικάω, conquer, overcome, overpower
ὄμμα, -ατος, τό, eye
ὄψις, -εως, ἡ, face; vision, eyesight, eye
πῶμα, -ατος, τό, drink
συναναίνω, συνανανῶ, dry up utterly
τις, τι, (gen. τινος), (indef. adj.) a, a certain
τρύπανον, τό, auger, drill
ὑπνώσσω, fall asleep
ὑπό (prep. + gen.), by
φαεσφόρος, -ον, light-bearing, bright
φάσγανον, τό, sword
χαλινός, ὁ, strap
χρή, it is necessary, one must (+ inf.)
ὡς (conj.), that
ὡσεί (adv.), just as

462-3 κυκλώσω...Κύκλωπος note *paronomasia* and *assonance*

φαεσφόρῳ...ὄψει "the monster's eye will be subjected to light in the form of scorching fire. Odysseus thus relishes the prospect of revenge on the monster with a pun and grimly ironic language." (O'Sullivan and Collard, 188)

463   κόρας pl. for sing.; cf. *Od.* 9.389

Χορός
>ἰοὺ ἰού·
465 γέγηθα μαινόμεσθα τοῖς εὑρήμασιν.

Ὀδυσσεύς
>κἄπειτα καὶ σὲ καὶ φίλους γέροντά τε
>νεὼς μελαίνης κοῖλον ἐμβήσας σκάφος
>διπλαῖσι κώπαις τῆσδ' ἀποστελῶ χθονός.

Χορός
>ἔστ' οὖν ὅπως ἂν ὡσπερεὶ σπονδῆς θεοῦ
470 κἀγὼ λαβοίμην τοῦ τυφλοῦντος ὄμματα
>δαλοῦ; φόνου γὰρ τοῦδε κοινωνεῖν θέλω.

Ὀδυσσεύς
>δεῖ γοῦν· μέγας γὰρ δαλός, οὗ ξυλληπτέον.

Χορός
>ὡς κἂν ἁμαξῶν ἑκατὸν ἀραίμην βάρος,
>εἰ τοῦ Κύκλωπος τοῦ κακῶς ὀλουμένου
475 ὀφθαλμὸν ὥσπερ σφηκιὰν ἐκθύψομεν.

---

465 γέγηθα μαινόμεσθα note *asyndeton* and shift from sing. to pl., both expressive of the satyrs' giddy excitement
γέγηθα 1st sing. perf. (w/ pres. sense) act. indic. < γηθέω
μαινόμεσθα = (poetic form of) μαινόμεθα
466 κἄπειτα = καὶ ἔπειτα
468 διπλαῖσι κώπαις dat. of means; most likely referring to two banks of oars on each side of the ship (i.e., a bireme)
469-70 ὡσπερεὶ σπονδῆς θεοῦ... i.e., just as I might do when taking hold of a drink-offering to the god
470 κἀγὼ = καὶ ἐγὼ
λαβοίμην 1st sing. aor. mid. opt. < λαμβάνω; potential opt.
ὄμματα see 463 and note ad loc.

αἴρω, lift (up)
ἅμαξα, ἡ, wagon
ἀποστέλλω, ἀποστελῶ, send away from (+ gen.)
βάρος, -ους, τό, weight
γέρων, -οντος, ὁ, old man
γηθέω, rejoice
γοῦν (particle), yes, in fact
δεῖ, it is necessary (+ inf.)
ἑκατόν (indecl.), hundred
ἐκτύφω, ἐκθύψω, smoke out
ἐμβαίνω, embark, go on board; (1st aor. ἐνέβησα) make to step in, put in, put on board
ἔπειτα (adv.), then
εὕρημα, -ατος, τό, invention
θέλω, wish, want (+ inf.)
ἰού (interjection; loud cry of sorrow, joy, or surprise)
κακῶς (adv.), horribly, miserably
κοῖλος, -η, -ον, hollow
κοινωνέω, have a share of, take part in (+ gen.)
κώπη, ἡ, oar-handle, oar
λαμβάνω, take; (mid.) take hold of (+ gen.)

μαίνομαι, be beside oneself w/ joy at, be crazy about (+ dat.)
μέγας, μεγάλη, μέγα, big, large
μέλας, μέλαινα, μέλαν, dark, black
ναῦς, νεώς, ἡ, ship
ξυλληπτέος, -η, -ον, to be taken hold of together (+ gen.)
ὄλλυμι, ruin, destroy
ὅπως (conj.), how, as; w/ ἔστιν, there is a way in which, it is possible that
ὀφθαλμός, ὁ, eye
σκάφος, -εος, τό, hull (of a ship)
σπονδή, ἡ, libation, drink-offering (of wine poured out to the gods before drinking)
σφηκιά, ἡ, wasp's nest
τυφλόω, blind
φόνος, ὁ, bloodshed, slaughter
χθών, χθονός, ἡ, land, country
ὥσπερ (adv.), just as
ὡσπερεί (adv.), just as if

---

472 μέγας γὰρ δαλός sc. ἐστι
 οὗ ξυλληπτέον sc. ἐστι; lit., "of which it is to be taken hold of together," i.e., "which we must take hold of together." ξυλληπτέον, a vb. adj. of ξυλλαμβάνω, expresses necessity (= δεῖ ξυλλαβεῖν)
473 ὡς "(You can be sure) that..." (Olson)
 κἂν = καὶ ἂν
 ἀραίμην 1st sing. aor. mid. (w/ same sense as act.) opt. < αἴρω; potential opt.
474 τοῦ κακῶς ὀλουμένου idiomatic curse phrase (lit., "of the one about to perish horribly") best rendered into English as: "that son of a bitch" (Olson) or "damned (Cyclops)" (O'Sullivan and Collard)

Ὀδυσσεύς
σιγᾶτέ νυν· δόλον γὰρ ἐξεπίστασαι·
χὤταν κελεύω, τοῖσιν ἀρχιτέκτοσιν
πείθεσθ'. ἐγὼ γὰρ ἄνδρας ἀπολιπὼν φίλους
τοὺς ἔνδον ὄντας οὐ μόνος σωθήσομαι.
480 [καίτοι φύγοιμ' ἂν κἀκβέβηκ' ἄντρου μυχῶν·
ἀλλ' οὐ δίκαιον ἀπολιπόντ' ἐμοὺς φίλους
ξὺν οἷσπερ ἦλθον δεῦρο σωθῆναι μόνον.]

Χορός
ἄγε, τίς πρῶτος, τίς δ' ἐπὶ πρώτῳ
ταχθεὶς δαλοῦ κώπην ὀχμάσαι
485 Κύκλωπος ἔσω βλεφάρων ὤσας
λαμπρὰν ὄψιν διακναίσει;
 (ᾠδὴ ἔνδοθεν)
σίγα σίγα. καὶ δὴ μεθύων
ἄχαριν κέλαδον μουσιζόμενος
490 σκαιὸς ἀπῳδὸς καὶ κλαυσόμενος
χωρεῖ πετρίνων ἔξω μελάθρων.

---

476 σιγᾶτέ...ἐξεπίστασαι note shift from pl. to sing. (cf. 440-1, 436, 466)
477 χὤταν = καὶ ὅταν [= ὅτε ἄν, "whenever" (+ subju.)]
478 τοῖσιν ἀρχιτέκτοσιν i.e., Odysseus and his men
479 σωθήσομαι 1st sing. fut. pass. < σώζω
480-2 Several editors suspect these verses as being a later interpolation because of both grammatical/syntactical and characterization issues. For the details, see Seaford 194 and O'Sullivan and Collard 191. As they stand, a lit. translation would be: "And yet I could flee, and I have come out of the recesses of the cave; but it is not right that I, leaving behind my friends with whom I came here, alone be saved."

ἄγε (impera. as adv.), come on!
ἀπολείπω, ἀπέλιπον, leave behind
ἀπῳδός, -όν, out of tune
ἀρχιτέκτων, -ονος, ὁ, director of works, architect
ἄχαρις, ἄχαρι, w/out grace or charm, unpleasant, disagreeable
βλέφαρον, τό, eyelid
διακναίω, grind out, destroy by scraping
δόλος, ὁ, stratagem, trick, plan
εἴσω/ἔσω (adv.; prep. + gen.), within, into
ἔνδοθεν (adv.), (from) within
ἔνδον (adv.), inside, within
ἐξεπίσταμαι, know (thoroughly)
ἔξω (adv./prep. + gen.), out of
ἐπί (prep. + dat.), after, behind
κέλαδος, ὁ, noise, din
κελεύω, order, command
κλαίω, κλαύσομαι, wail, cry, howl; (freq. in Attic, fut. "shall howl" = "shall pay dearly")

κώπη, ἡ, handle
λαμπρός, -ά, -όν, bright
μεθύω, be drunk
μέλαθρον, -ου, τό, main beam which supports the ceiling, roof; (mostly in pl. =) house, hall(s)
μόνος, -η, -ον, alone
μουσίζω (mid. w/ act. sense), sing
ὀχμάζω, grip tightly
πείθω, persuade; (mid.) obey, listen to (+ dat.)
πέτρινος, -η, -ον, rocky
πρῶτος, -η, -ον, first
σιγάω, keep silence, be quiet
σώζω, save
τίς, τί (gen. τίνος; interrog. pron. and adj.), who? which? what?
τάσσω, station, post
σκαιός, -ά, -όν, gauche, uncouth (lit., left-handed)
χωρέω, come
ᾠδή, ἡ, song, inging
ὠθέω, ἔωσα, thrust, push

---

483 τίς πρῶτος sc. will be stationed
ἐπὶ πρώτῳ lit., "after the first," i.e., "second"

484 ταχθεὶς masc. nom. sing. aor. pass. part. < τάσσω
ὀχμάσαι "The infin. depends on the notion of will or desire implicit in ταχθείς; "stationed here so that he might...."" (Olson, 61)

485 ἔσω βλεφάρων i.e., in his eye; note the pl., which Homer himself always uses to describe the Cyclops' one eye

487 An ancient stage direction, though not apparently written by Euripides

487 καὶ δή "and what is more"; this phrase "introduces a still stronger reason for silence" (Long, 34)

φέρε νιν κώμοις παιδεύσωμεν
τὸν ἀπαίδευτον·
πάντως μέλλει τυφλὸς εἶναι.

495 μάκαρ ὅστις εὐιάζει
βοτρύων φίλαισι πηγαῖς
ἐπὶ κῶμον ἐκπετασθεὶς
φίλον ἄνδρ' ὑπαγκαλίζων
ἐπὶ δεμνίοισί τ' ἄνθος
500 χλιδανᾶς ἔχων ἑταίρας,
μυρόχριστος λιπαρὸν βό-
στρυχον, αὐδᾷ δέ· Θύραν τίς οἴξει μοι;

Κύκλωψ

παπαπαῖ· πλέως μὲν οἴνου,
γάνυμαι <δὲ> δαιτὸς ἥβᾳ,
505 σκάφος ὁλκὰς ὣς γεμισθεὶς
ποτὶ σέλμα γαστρὸς ἄκρας.

---

492 **φέρε** + subju. is a colloquialism
κώμοις dat. of means
παιδεύσωμεν 1st pl. aor. act. subju. < παιδεύω; hortatory subju.
495 **μάκαρ** sc. ἐστι
496-7 An impressionistic image of the reveler as sailor, spreading out his sails on "seas of wine" as he sets off to the revel
496 **ἐπὶ κῶμον** "(off) to the revel"
497 **ἐκπετασθεὶς** masc. nom. sing. aor. pass. part. < ἐκπετάννυμι; the pass. part. both describes the relaxed bodily position of the intoxicated reveler and, as noted above, conveys the image of him having spread his sails to the winds, i.e., giving himself completely over to X (dat.)

ἄκρος, -α, -ον, topmost
ἄνθος, -ους, τό, blossom, flower, youthful bloom
ἀπαίδευτος, -ον, uneducated, ignorant, boorish
αὐδάω, say, speak
βόστρυχος, ὁ, hair
βότρυς, -υος, ὁ, bunch of grapes, grape-cluster
γάνυμαι, be happy or rejoice at (+ dat.)
γαστήρ, -τρός, ἡ, belly
γεμίζω, fill full of, loard or freight w/ (a cargo of a ship)
δαίς, δαιτός, ἡ, banquet, feast
δέμνιον, τό, (mostly in pl.) bed
ἐκπετάννυμι, spread out (a sail or wings); (pass.) wholly given up or over to (+ dat.)
ἑταίρα, ἡ, courtesan, high-class prostitute
εὐιάζω/εὐάζω, cry euoi (to Bacchus/Dionysus)
ἥβη, ἡ, youthful cheer, passion, or zest
θύρα, ἡ, door
κῶμος, ὁ, revel; drinking song
λιπαρός, -ά, -όν, shining (w/ oil), sleek

μάκαρ (gen. -αρος), μάκαιρα, happy, blessed
μέλλω, be about to, going to (+ inf.)
μυρόχριστος, -ον, anointed w/ perfumed or scented oil
νιν (Doric and Tragic acc. 3rd pers. sing. pron. = αὐτόν, αὐτήν)
οἴγω, open
οἶνος, ὁ, wine
ὁλκάς, -άδος, ἡ, cargo-ship
ὅστις, ἥτις, ὅ τι, anyone who, anything which
παιδεύω, educate
πάντως (adv.), in any case, at any rate, anyway
παπαπαῖ (exclamation of suffering, surprise or satisfaction)
πηγή, ἡ, stream
πλέως, πλέα, πλέων, full of, filled w/ (+ gen.)
ποτί (= πρός)
σέλμα, -ατος, τό, deck
τυφλός, -ή, -όν, blind
ὑπαγκαλίζω, embrace
φέρε (impera. as adv.), come!
φίλος, -η, -ον, dear, beloved
χλιδανός, -ή, -όν, voluptuous
ὡς (adv.), like

498-502 The satyrs' song turns to the sexual aspects of the banquet/revel, both (potentially) homo- (498) and (definitely) heterosexual (499-502)

501-2 λιπαρὸν βόστρυχον acc. of respect

502 Θύραν τίς οἴξει μοι; words spoken in a traditional love-song sung by a man in the street to a woman in her house

505 σκάφος acc. of respect
ὁλκὰς ὥς i.e., w/ a full cargo of wine; the accent on ὥς indicates that it is to be taken w/ the word that precedes it
γεμισθεὶς masc. nom. sing. aor. pass. part. < γεμίζω

ὑπάγει μ' ὁ φόρτος εὔφρων
ἐπὶ κῶμον ἦρος ὥραις
ἐπὶ Κύκλωπας ἀδελφούς.
510 φέρε μοι, ξεῖνε, φέρ', ἀσκὸν ἔνδος μοι.

Χορός

καλὸν ὄμμασιν δεδορκὼς
καλὸς ἐκπερᾷ μελάθρων
⟨κελαδῶν·⟩ Φιλεῖ τις ἡμᾶς.
λύχνα δ' ἀμμένειν ἔασον·
515 †χρόα χὼς† τέρεινα νύμφα
δροσερῶν ἔσωθεν ἄντρων.
στεφάνων δ' οὐ μία χροιὰ
περὶ σὸν κρᾶτα τάχ' ἐξομιλήσει.

Ὀδυσσεύς

Κύκλωψ, ἄκουσον· ὡς ἐγὼ τοῦ Βακχίου
520 τούτου τρίβων εἴμ', ὃν πιεῖν ἔδωκά σοι.

Κύκλωψ

ὁ Βάκχιος δὲ τίς; θεὸς νομίζεται;

Ὀδυσσεύς

μέγιστος ἀνθρώποισιν ἐς τέρψιν βίου.

---

509 ὥραις pl. for sing.; dat. of time when
510 Addressed to Odysseus
511-17 Heavily sarcastic version of a traditional wedding song, w/ the Cyclops as groom
511 Both "looking a lovely (look) w/ his eyes" (i.e., giving a lover's glance [to someone]) and "looking lovely in appearance"
513 ἡμᾶς pl. for sing. (an example of *pluralis maiestatis*)

ἀδελφός, ὁ, brother
ἀμμένω (poetic from of ἀναμένω), await, wait for
ἄνθρωπος, ὁ, person, human
ἀσκός, ὁ, wine-skin
βίος, ὁ, life
δέρκομαι, look; (perf. part.) having sight (opposite of τυφλός)
δίδωμι, ἔδωκα, give
δροσερός, -ά, -όν, dewy
ἐάω, allow, permit; let alone, let be (+ acc.), let X (acc.) go
εἰς/ἐς (prep. + acc.), for
εἷς, μία, ἕν, (gen. ἑνός, μιᾶς, ἑνός), one
ἐκπεράω, come out of (+ gen.)
ἐνδίδωμι, give or put into one's hands, give X (acc.) to Y (dat.), surrender X (acc.) to Y (dat.)
ἐξομιλέω, accompany, keep one company
ἔσωθεν (adv./prep. + gen.), within
εὔφρων, -ον, cheerful
ἦρ, ἦρος, τό, spring

καλός, -ή, -όν, fine, beautiful, lovely
κελαδέω, shout, cry
κράς, κρατός, ἡ, head
λύχνος, ὁ, (pl. either οἱ λύχνοι or τὰ λύχνα) lamp
μέγιστος, -η, -ον, greatest
νομίζω, consider as, acknowledge as
νύμφη, ἡ, bride; nymph
ὄμμα, -ατος, τό, eye; (pl. sometimes =) face, appearance
στέφανος, ὁ, garland, crown
τάχα (adv.), quickly, soon
τέρην, -εινα, -εν, tender
τέρψις, -εως, ἡ, joy, delight, pleasure, enjoyment
τρίβων, -ωνος, ὁ/ἡ, old hand, someone w/ experience w/ or in (+ gen.)
ὑπάγω, guide, lead, bring
φιλέω/φιλῶ, love
φόρτος, ὁ, cargo
χροιά, ἡ, color
ὥρα, ἡ, season
ὡς (conj.), since

---

514 "i.e., "do not await the lamps!", referring to the lamps that lit the bridal chamber." (Olson, 63)
λύχνα...ἀμμένειν the inf. phrase is the dir. obj. of ἔασον
ἔασον 2nd sing. aor. act. impera. < ἐάω
515 †χρόα χώς† the text seems irremediably corrupt; for further details, see Seaford 191-2 and O'Sullivan and Collard 196-7
515-16 τέρεινα νύμφα...ἔσωθεν sc. ἐστι
νύμφα = (Doric form of) νύμφη
517-18 "superficially an allusion to elaborate wedding-wreathes (normally made of a wide variety of flowers), but also a reference to the bloody blinding to come (S)." (Olson, 63)
520 πιεῖν epexegetical (i.e., explanatory) inf.
521 τίς sc. ἐστι

Κύκλωψ

ἐρυγγάνω γοῦν αὐτὸν ἡδέως ἐγώ.

Ὀδυσσεύς

τοιόσδ' ὁ δαίμων· οὐδένα βλάπτει βροτῶν.

Κύκλωψ

525 θεὸς δ' ἐν ἀσκῷ πῶς γέγηθ' οἴκους ἔχων;

Ὀδυσσεύς

ὅπου τιθῇ τις, ἐνθάδ' ἐστὶν εὐπετής.

Κύκλωψ

οὐ τοὺς θεοὺς χρῆν σῶμ' ἔχειν ἐν δέρμασιν.

Ὀδυσσεύς

τί δ', εἴ σε τέρπει γ'; ἢ τὸ δέρμα σοι πικρόν;

Κύκλωψ

μισῶ τὸν ἀσκόν· τὸ δὲ ποτὸν φιλῶ τόδε.

Ὀδυσσεύς

530 μένων νυν αὐτοῦ πῖνε κεὐθύμει, Κύκλωψ.

Κύκλωψ

οὐ χρή μ' ἀδελφοῖς τοῦδε προσδοῦναι ποτοῦ;

Ὀδυσσεύς

ἔχων γὰρ αὐτὸς τιμιώτερος φανῇ.

Κύκλωψ

διδοὺς δὲ τοῖς φίλοισι χρησιμώτερος.

Ὀδυσσεύς

πυγμὰς ὁ κῶμος λοίδορόν τ' ἔριν φιλεῖ.

---

524   τοιόσδ' ὁ δαίμων sc. ἐστι
525   γέγηθ' 3rd sing. perf. (w/ pres. sense) act. indic. < γηθέω
526   ὅπου = ὅπου ἄν (+ subju.); in drama, ἄν is often omitted

αὐτός, -ή, -ό, (intensive adj.) -self; (pl.) -selves
αὐτοῦ (adv.), here
βλάπτω, harm
βροτός, ὁ, mortal man
γηθέω, rejoice in, enjoy (+ part.)
γοῦν (particle), yes, certainly; at any rate
δαίμων, -ονος, ὁ/ἡ, divine power, divinity
δέρμα, -ατος, τό, skin, hide
ἐνθάδε (adv.), there
ἔρις, -ιδος, (acc. ἔριν) ἡ, quarreling
ἐρυγγάνω, belch up
εὐθυμέω, be cheerful, enjoy oneself
εὐπετής, -ές, contented, at ease
ἤ (conj.), or
ἡδέως (adv.), w/ pleasure
λοίδορος, -ον, abusive
μένω, stay
μισέω/μισῶ, hate
νυν (adv.), then
οἶκος, ὁ, house
ὅπου (adv.), wherever

οὐδείς, οὐδεμία, οὐδέν, no one, nobody, nothing
πικρός, -ά, -όν, unpleasant
πίνω, ἔπιον (aor.), drink
πότος, ὁ, drink
προσδίδωμι, give a share of, give some of (+ gen.)
πυγμή, ἡ, fist-fight, fight
πῶς (adv.), how?
σῶμα, -ατος, τό, body
τέρπω, delight, gladden
τίθημι, put
τιμιώτερος, -η, -ον, more honored
τις, τι, (gen. τινος), (indef. pron.) anyone, anything; someone, something; some, a certain
τοιόσδε, -άδε, -όνδε, such, of such a kind
φαίνω, bring to light; (mid./pass.) be seen (to be), appear (to be)
φίλος, ὁ, friend, kin
χρή, it is necessary, should or ought one (dat.) to do X (inf.)
χρησιμώτερος, -η, -ον, more useful or helpful

---

526 τιθῇ sc. αὐτόν
527 χρῆν = (unaugmented form of) ἐχρῆν
ἐν δέρμασιν "Normally only peasants and the poor dressed in animal skins (S)" (Olson, 63)
528 τί δ' "But what (of it)?"
τὸ δέρμα σοι πικρόν sc. ἐστι
530 κεὐθύμει = καὶ εὐθύμει
531 προσδοῦναι aor. act. inf. < προσδίδωμι
532 γὰρ "no, for/because"
φανῇ 2nd sing. fut. mid. < φαίνω
533 τοῖς φίλοισι χρησιμώτερος sc. φανοῦμαι

Κύκλωψ
535 μεθύω μέν, ἔμπας δ' οὔτις ἂν ψαύσειέ μου.
Ὀδυσσεύς
ὦ τᾶν, πεπωκότ' ἐν δόμοισι χρὴ μένειν.
Κύκλωψ
ἠλίθιος ὅστις μὴ πιὼν κῶμον φιλεῖ.
Ὀδυσσεύς
ὃς δ' ἂν μεθυσθείς γ' ἐν δόμοις μείνῃ σοφός.
Κύκλωψ
τί δρῶμεν, ὦ Σιληνέ; σοὶ μένειν δοκεῖ;
Σιληνός
540 δοκεῖ· τί γὰρ δεῖ συμποτῶν ἄλλων, Κύκλωψ;
Ὀδυσσεύς
καὶ μὴν λαχνῶδές γ' οὖδας ἀνθηρᾶς χλόης.
Σιληνός
καὶ πρός γε θάλπος ἡλίου πίνειν καλόν.
κλίθητί νύν μοι πλευρὰ θεὶς ἐπὶ χθονός.
Κύκλωψ
ἰδού.
545 τί δῆτα τὸν κρατῆρ' ὄπισθ' ἐμοῦ τίθης;
Σιληνός
ὡς μὴ παριών τις καταβάλῃ.

---

535 οὔτις an allusion to Odysseus' famous Οὖτις joke (see 549)
ψαύσειέ 3rd sing. aor. act. opt. < ψαύω; potential opt.
536 πεπωκότ' masc. acc. sing. perf. act. part. < πίνω
537 ἠλίθιος sc. ἐστι
μὴ...φιλεῖ μὴ (= οὐ) governs φιλεῖ
538 μεθυσθείς masc. nom. sing. aor. pass. part. < μεθύσκω

104

ἀλλός, -ή, -ό, other
ἀνθηρός, -ά, -όν, blooming
δεῖ, there is need of (+ gen.)
δῆτα (adv.; in questions, mostly to mark an inference or consequence, sometimes expressing indignation), then
δοκεῖ, it seems (good) to X (dat.)
δόμος, ὁ, house (pl. often = sing., esp. in verse)
δράω, do
ἔμπας (adv.), yet, even so
ἠλίθιος, -α, -ον, foolish
ἥλιος, ὁ, sun
θάλπος, -εος, τό, warmth
καταβάλλω, κατέβαλον, knock down
κλίνω, make to recline; (pass.) lie down
κρατήρ, -ῆρος, ὁ, mixing bowl (in which wine was mixed w/ water) λαχνώδης, -ες, downy (+ gen.)
μεθύσκω, make drunk; (pass.) be or get drunk, be intoxicated
μεθύω, be drunk

μήν (particle), in fact, in truth; καὶ μήν introduces a new fact or argument
ὄπισθεν (adv./prep. + gen.), behind
ὅστις, ἥτις, ὅ τι, anyone who, anything which
οὖδας, οὖδεος, τό, ground
οὔτις, οὔτι, no one, nothing
πάρειμι, pass by
πλευρόν, τό, rib; (pl.) side
σοφός, -ή, -όν, wise
συμπότης, -ου, ὁ, fellow-drinker, banqueter
τᾶν, (indecl. noun only in Attic and only in phrase ὦ τᾶν, as a form of either polite or condescending address) my good friend; hey, fella
χθών, χθονός, ἡ, ground
χλόη, ἡ, foliage, the first green shoots of plants in spring
ψαύω, touch or lay hands upon (+ gen.)
ὡς (conj.), in order that (+ subju.)

---

538 μείνῃ 3rd sing. aor. act. subju. < μένω
    σοφός sc. ἐστι
539 δρῶμεν 1st pl. pres. act. subju. < δράω; deliberative subju.
540 δοκεῖ sc. μοι
541 "i.e., "there is abundant grass and flowers (to lie down in)." (Olson, 64)
542 καλόν sc. ἐστι
543 κλίθητί 2nd sing. aor. pass. impera. < κλίνω
    μοι dat. of feeling (aka ethical dat.), i.e., "please"
    θείς masc. nom. sing. aor. act. part. < τίθημι
544 ἰδού impera. of εἶδον ("look!" < ὁράω/ὁρῶ) is often used as adv., "see, (I did it)" (a colloquial usage)
545 τί δῆτα "Why then (if you want me to lie down)...?"
546 μὴ...καταβάλῃ μή governs καταβάλῃ

Κύκλωψ
πίνειν μὲν οὖν
κλέπτων σὺ βούλῃ· κάτθες αὐτὸν ἐς μέσον.
σὺ δ', ὦ ξέν', εἰπὲ τοὔνομ' ὅ τι σε χρὴ καλεῖν.
Ὀδυσσεύς
Οὖτιν· χάριν δὲ τίνα λαβών σ' ἐπαινέσω;
Κύκλωψ
550 πάντων σ' ἑταίρων ὕστερον θοινάσομαι.
Σιληνός
καλόν γε τὸ γέρας τῷ ξένῳ δίδως, Κύκλωψ.
Κύκλωψ
οὗτος, τί δρᾷς; τὸν οἶνον ἐκπίνεις λάθρᾳ;
Σιληνός
οὔκ, ἀλλ' ἔμ' οὗτος ἔκυσεν ὅτι καλὸν βλέπω.
Κύκλωψ
κλαύσῃ, φιλῶν τὸν οἶνον οὐ φιλοῦντα σέ.
Σιληνός
555 οὐ μὰ Δί', ἐπεί μού φησ' ἐρᾶν ὄντος καλοῦ.
Κύκλωψ
ἔγχει, πλέων δὲ τὸν σκύφον δίδου μόνον.
Σιληνός
πῶς οὖν κέκραται; φέρε διασκεψώμεθα.

---

546 μὲν οὖν "to the contrary," i.e., "no"
546-7 πίνειν...κλέπτων sc. it, i.e., the κρατήρ filled w/ wine
547 κάτθες 2nd sing. syncopated aor. act. impera. < κατατίθημι
ἐς μέσον i.e., between us
548-50 Cf. *Od.* 9.355-70

βλέπω, look
βούλομαι, wish, want
γέρας, -αος, τό, gift, present
διασκέπτομαι, examine, consider carefully
ἐγχέω, pour in
ἐκπίνω, drink (deeply)
ἐπαινέω, praise, compliment publically
ἐπεί (conj.), since, seeing that
ἐράω, love, be love w/ (+ gen.)
ἑταῖρος, ὁ, comrade, companion
Ζεύς, Διός, Διΐ, Δία, ὁ, Zeus
θοινάω, feast on, eat
καλέω, call
κατατίθημι, place or put down
κλαίω, κλαύσομαι, wail, cry, howl; (freq. in Attic, fut. "shall howl" = "shall pay dearly")
κλέπτω, steal
κυνέω, kiss

λάθρῃ (adv.), secretly, in secret
λαμβάνω, ἔλαβον, get, receive
κεράννυμι, mix
μά (particle used in strong protestations and oaths), by (+ acc. of deity appealed to)
μέσον, τό, middle
μόνον (adv.), only
οἶνος, ὁ, wine
ὄνομα, -ατος, τό, name
ὅστις, ἥτις, ὅ τι, who, which
ὅτι (particle), because
πᾶς, πᾶσα, πᾶν, all, every
πλέως, πλέα, πλέων, full
σκύφος, ὁ, cup
τίς, τί (gen. τίνος; interrog. pron. and adj.), who? which? what?
ὕστερος, -α, -ον, last
φέρε (impera. as adv.), come!
φημί, say
χάρις, χάριτος, ἡ, favor

---

548 τοὔνομ' = τὸ ὄνομα
549 Οὖτιν (nom. Οὖτις) Odysseus intends the drunken Cyclops to mistake the invented name for οὔτις ("nobody," "no one")
552 οὗτος "Hey, you!"; addressed to Silenus, this use of οὗτος is emphatic, most often in a contemptuous sense
553 οὗτος sc. οἶνος
     ἔκυσεν = (poetic form of) ἐκύνησεν
     καλὸν βλέπω cf. 511
554 κλαύσῃ cf. 490
556 ἔγχει 2nd sing. pres. act. impera. < ἐγχέω
     πλέων...μόνον "only (when it's) full"
     δίδου 2nd sing. pres. act. impera. < δίδωμι; sc. μοι
557 The Cyclops is (rather fastidiously) inquiring into the proportion of water to wine
     κέκραται 3rd sing. perf. pass. indic. < κεράννυμι; sc. οἶνος as subj.
     διασκεψώμεθα 1st pl. aor. mid. (dep.) subju. < διασκέπτομαι; hortatory subju.

Κύκλωψ
ἀπολεῖς· δὸς οὕτως.

Σιληνός
οὐ μὰ Δί, οὐ πρὶν ἄν γέ σε
στέφανον ἴδω λαβόντα γεύσωμαί τ' ἔτι.

Κύκλωψ
560   οἰνοχόος ἄδικος.

Σιληνός
⟨ναὶ⟩ μὰ Δί, ἀλλ' οἶνος γλυκύς.
ἀπομακτέον δέ σοὐστὶν ὡς λήψῃ πιεῖν.

Κύκλωψ
ἰδού, καθαρὸν τὸ χεῖλος αἱ τρίχες τέ μου.

Σιληνός
θές νυν τὸν ἀγκῶν' εὐρύθμως κᾆτ' ἔκπιε,
ὥσπερ μ' ὁρᾷς πίνοντα—χὥσπερ οὐκέτι.

Κύκλωψ
565   ἆ ἆ, τί δράσεις;

Σιληνός
ἡδέως ἠμύστισα.

---

558   ἀπολεῖς sc. με (i.e., "You'll be the death of me!") or τὸν οἶνον (i.e., "you are mixing the wine w/ the wrong proportions/ruining it")
δὸς 2nd sing. aor. act. impera. < δίδωμι; sc. μοι
πρὶν ἄν "until" (+ subju., usu. aor.)

559   ἴδω 1st sing. aor. act. subju. < ὁράω/εἶδον
λαβόντα i.e., wearing
γεύσωμαί τ' ἔτι probably spoken as an aside to the audience
γεύσωμαί 1st sing. aor. mid. subju. < γεύω

ἆ (exclamation expressing envy, pity, contempt or outrage), ah!
ἀγκών, -ῶνος, ὁ, elbow, arm
ἄδικος, -ον, unjust, not fair
ἀμυστίζω, ἠμύστισα, chug, drink a cup w/out taking a breath
ἀπόλλυμι, ἀπολῶ, ruin, destroy
ἀπομακτέος, -η, -ον, to be wiped off
γεύω, give a taste; (mid.) taste
γλυκύς, -εῖα, -ύ, sweet
εἶτα (adv.), then
ἔτι (adv.), still more
εὐρύθμως (adv.), gracefully

ἡδέως (adv.), w/ pleasure
θρίξ, τριχός, ἡ, hair
καθαρός, -ά, -όν, clean
λαμβάνω, λήψομαι, take, receive
ναί (adv.), yes
νυν (adv.), then
οἰνοχόος, ὁ, wine pourer
οὐκέτι (adv.), no longer
οὕτως (adv.), at once
στέφανος, ὁ, garland, crown
τίθημι, put, place
χεῖλος, -εος, τό, lip
ὡς (conj.), so that, in order that (+ fut. indic.)
ὥσπερ (adv.), just as

---

560 οἰνοχόος ἄδικος sc. ἐστι
οἰνοχόος = ὁ οἰνοχόος
οἶνος γλυκύς sc. ἐστι
οἶνος = ὁ οἶνος

561 ἀπομακτέον δέ σούστὶν lit., "But it is to be wiped off for you," i.e., "you need to wipe your mouth/face"
ἀπομακτέον, a vb. adj. of ἀπομάσσω/ἀπομάττω, expresses necessity (= δεῖ ἀπομάξαι)
σούστὶν = σοι ἐστὶν
λήψῃ sc. τὸν οἶνον or τὸν σκύφον
πιεῖν epexegetic (i.e., explanatory) inf.

562 καθαρὸν τὸ χεῖλος αἱ τρίχες τέ sc. εἰσι
αἱ τρίχες i.e., his beard

563 θές...εὐρύθμως i.e., put your left elbow on the ground (since the right hand will be used to hold the cup)
θές 2nd sing. aor. act. impera. < τίθημι
κᾆτ' = καὶ εἶτα

564 χὥσπερ = καὶ ὥσπερ

565 ἠμύστισα cf. 417
χὥσπερ οὐκέτι sc. μ' ὁρᾷς πίνοντα; i.e., at this point Silenus "drinks, tipping the wine cup up so as to be invisible behind it" (Kovacs, 125)

Κύκλωψ
   λάβ', ὦ ξέν', αὐτὸς οἰνοχόος τέ μοι γενοῦ.
Ὀδυσσεύς
   γιγνώσκεται γοῦν ἄμπελος τῇμῇ χερί.
Κύκλωψ
   φέρ' ἔγχεόν νυν.
Ὀδυσσεύς
                  ἐγχέω, σίγα μόνον.
Κύκλωψ
   χαλεπὸν τόδ' εἶπας, ὅστις ἂν πίνῃ πολύν.
Ὀδυσσεύς
570 ἰδού· λαβὼν ἔκπιθι καὶ μηδὲν λίπῃς·
   συνεκθανεῖν δὲ σπῶντα χρὴ τῷ πώματι.
Κύκλωψ
   παπαῖ, σοφόν γε τὸ ξύλον τῆς ἀμπέλου.
Ὀδυσσεύς
   κἂν μὲν σπάσῃς γε δαιτὶ πρὸς πολλῇ πολύν,
   τέγξας ἄδιψον νηδύν, εἰς ὕπνον βαλεῖ,
575 ἢν δ' ἐλλίπῃς τι, ξηρανεῖ σ' ὁ Βάκχιος.
Κύκλωψ
   ἰοὺ ἰού·
   ὡς ἐξένευσα μόγις· ἄκρατος ἡ χάρις.

---

566 γενοῦ 2nd sing. aor. mid. (dep.) impera. < γίγνομαι
567 ἄμπελος = ἡ ἄμπελος; i.e., wine
   τῇμῇ χερί = τῇ ἐμῇ χερί (= poetic form of χειρί); dat. of agent w/ pass. vb.
568 ἔγχεόν 2nd sing. aor. act. impera. < ἐγχέω
569 "This thing you said (is) difficult (to do for) anyone who..."

ἄδιψος, -ον, not thirsty
ἄκρατος, -ον, unmixed, pure
ἄμπελος, ἡ, grape-vine
αὐτός, -ή, -ό, (intensive adj.) -self; (pl.) -selves
βάλλω, βαλῶ, put, send
γίγνομαι, be
γιγνώσκω, recognize, know
γοῦν (particle), yes, certainly; at any rate, at least
δαίς, δαιτός, ἡ, meal, food
ἐκνέω, ἐξένευσα, escape by swimming
ἐλλείπω, ἐνέλιπον, leave (behind)
ἰού (interjection; loud cry of sorrow, joy, or surprise)
λείπω, leave
μόγις (adv.), barely, scarcely
νηδύς, -ύος, ἡ, stomach, belly
ξηραίνω, ξηρανῶ, dry X (acc.) up, make X (acc.) parched

ξύλον, τό, wood
παπαῖ (exclamation of suffering, surprise or satisfaction)
πολύς, πολλή, πολύ, much; (pl.) many
πρός (prep. + dat.), on top of, in addition to, along w/
πῶμα, -ατος, τό, drink
σιγάω, keep silence, be quiet
σοφός, -ή, -όν, clever
σπάω, gulp down, drain
συνεκθνήσκω, expire along w/ (+ dat.), pass out along w/ (+ dat.)
τέγγω, wet, soak, drench
ὕπνος, ὁ, sleep
χαλεπός, -ή, -όν, difficult
χάρις, ἡ, delight
χείρ, χειρός, ἡ, hand
χρή, it is necessary that X (acc.) do Y (inf.)
ὡς (exclamation), how!

---

569 πίνῃ subju. in an indef. rel. cl.
πολύν sc. οἶνον here and at 573
570 ἔκπιθι 2nd sing. aor. act. impera. < ἐκπίνω
λίπῃς 2nd sing. aor. act. subju. < λείπω; prohibitive subju. (w/ μηδέν)
571 συνεκθανεῖν aor. act. inf. < συνεκθνήσκω
572 σοφόν...ἀμπέλου "i.e., because it has produced this wonderful invention, wine." (Olson, 67)
573 κἂν = καὶ ἐάν [= εἰ ἄν], "even if" (+ subju.)
574 τέγξας ἄδιψον νηδύν cf. 326. ἄδιψον is a predicative-proleptic adj., i.e., "the belly (so that it is) not thirsty"
βαλεῖ subj. = οἶνος, obj. = "the one drinking"
575 ἢν = ἐάν [= εἰ ἄν], "if (ever)" (+ subju.)
577 ὡς ἐξένευσα μόγις "frequently the wine in drinking cups was likened to the sea with painted ships on the inside of the lip of the cup which would appear to float on the surface of the wine..." (O'Sullivan and Collard, 205)

ὁ δ' οὐρανός μοι συμμεμιγμένος δοκεῖ
τῇ γῇ φέρεσθαι, τοῦ Διός τε τὸν θρόνον
580 λεύσσω τὸ πᾶν τε δαιμόνων ἁγνὸν σέβας.
οὐκ ἂν φιλήσαιμ'· αἱ Χάριτες πειρῶσί με.
ἅλις· Γανυμήδη τόνδ' ἔχων ἀναπαύσομαι
κάλλιον ἢ τὰς Χάριτας. ἥδομαι δέ πως
τοῖς παιδικοῖσι μᾶλλον ἢ τοῖς θήλεσιν.

Σιληνός
585 ἐγὼ γὰρ ὁ Διός εἰμι Γανυμήδης, Κύκλωψ;

Κύκλωψ
ναὶ μὰ Δί', ὃν ἁρπάζω γ' ἐγὼ 'κ τῆς Δαρδάνου.

Σιληνός
ἀπόλωλα, παῖδες· σχέτλια πείσομαι κακά.

Κύκλωψ
μέμφῃ τὸν ἐραστὴν κἀντρυφᾷς πεπωκότι;

Σιληνός
οἴμοι· πικρότατον οἶνον ὄψομαι τάχα.

---

578 συμμεμιγμένος masc. nom. sing. perf. mid./pass. part. < συμμίγνυμι
579 φέρεσθαι sc. before my eyes
579-80 τοῦ Διός... σέβας the Cyclops' hallucination allows him to make an abrupt volte-face of his earlier contemptuous views of Zeus (and, by extension, the Olympian gods) as expressed in 318-21. This intoxicated revelation will, however, prove very short-lived
581 φιλήσαιμ' 1st sing. aor. act. opt. < φιλέω; potential opt. in an interrogative wish; sc. them, i.e., the chorus of satyrs, whom he imagines to be the Graces (three female divinities who were the attendants of Aphrodite)
582 ἅλις addressed to the allegedly flirtatious chorus of satyrs

ἁγνός, -ή, -όν, holy
ἅλις (adv.), enough! stop it!
ἀναπαύω, ἀναπαύσομαι, rest, sleep (the vb. also has sexual connotations; cf. English "go to bed/sleep with")
ἀπόλλυμι, destroy utterly; (perf. act.) be done for, be lost
ἁρπάζω, seize, snatch away
Γανυμήδης, -ους, ὁ, Ganymede
γῆ, ἡ, land, earth
δαίμων, -ονος, ὁ/ἡ, divine power, divinity
Δάρδανος, ὁ, Dardanus (son of Zeus and founder of Troy)
δοκέω, seem
ἐντρυφάω, turn up one's nose at, treat haughtily (+ dat.)
ἐραστής, -οῦ, ὁ, lover
ἤ (conj.), than
ἥδομαι, take pleasure in (+ dat.)
θῆλυς, θήλεια, θῆλυ, female
θρόνος, ὁ, throne
κακά, τά, evils, misfortunes, ills
κάλλιον (adv.), more splendidly

λεύσσω, see
μᾶλλον (adv.), more
μέμφομαι, find fault w/ (+ acc.)
οἴμοι (exclamation of pain, fright, pity, anger, grief, or surprise)
ὁράω/ὁρῶ, ὄψομαι, see
οὐρανός, ὁ, heaven, sky
παιδικός, -ή, -όν, of a child, boyish; τὰ παιδικά, "boyish things," i.e., "boys" (τὰ παιδικά often means sing. "boyfriend")
παῖς, παιδός, ὁ, son, child
πάσχω, πείσομαι, suffer
πειράω, tempt
πικρότατος, -α, -ον, most bitter
πίνω, drink; (perf.) be drunk
πως (particle), somehow
σέβας, τό, majesty
συμμίγνυμι, mix together w/ (+ dat.)
σχέτλιος, -α, -ον, cruel, savage; miserable
τάχα (adv.), soon
φιλέω, kiss
Χάρις, Χάριτος, ἡ, Grace

---

582 Γανυμήδη the "joke" comes from the Cyclops' drunken misidentification of Silenus as Ganymede, a very young (and very attractive) Trojan prince whom Zeus, in the form of an eagle, snatched away to Olympus to pour his wine and be his paramour
ἔχων the pres. part. of ἔχω approaches the meaning of the English prep. "with"
584 τοῖς θήλεσιν i.e., women
585 γὰρ "(are you saying this) because...?" (Olson, 67)
586 'κ τῆς = ἐκ τῆς γῆς
587 ἀπόλωλα 1st sing. perf. (= pres.) act. indic. < ἀπόλλυμι
588 κἀντρυφᾷς = καὶ ἐντρυφᾷς
πεπωκότι masc. dat. sing. perf. act. part. < πίνω

Ὀδυσσεύς

590 ἄγε δή, Διονύσου παῖδες, εὐγενῆ τέκνα,
ἔνδον μὲν ἀνήρ· τῷ δ' ὕπνῳ παρειμένος
τάχ' ἐξ ἀναιδοῦς φάρυγος ὠθήσει κρέα.
δαλὸς δ' ἔσωθεν αὐλίων πνέων καπνὸν
παρευτρέπισται, κοὐδὲν ἄλλο πλὴν πυροῦν
595 Κύκλωπος ὄψιν· ἀλλ' ὅπως ἀνὴρ ἔσῃ.

Χορός

πέτρας τὸ λῆμα κἀδάμαντος ἕξομεν.
χώρει δ' ἐς οἴκους πρίν τι τὸν πατέρα παθεῖν
ἀπάλαμνον· ὡς σοι τἀνθάδ' ἐστὶν εὐτρεπῆ.

Ὀδυσσεύς

Ἥφαιστ', ἄναξ Αἰτναῖε, γείτονος κακοῦ
600 λαμπρὸν πυρώσας ὄμμ' ἀπαλλάχθηθ' ἅπαξ,
σύ τ', ὦ μελαίνης Νυκτὸς ἐκπαίδευμ', Ὕπνε,

---

590 Διονύσου παῖδες since the satyrs are not technically the "sons" of Dionysus, Odysseus seems to be flattering them (note too his use of the nearly synonymous phrase εὐγενῆ τέκνα in *apposition*), for "their actual father Silenus (16, 269, etc.) is hardly an appropriate role model to be invoked (especially in the current circumstances!), compared to their patron god who was at least pre-eminent in the Gigantomachy..." (O'Sullivan and Collard, 208)

591 ἔνδον μὲν ἀνήρ = ἔνδον μὲν ὁ ἀνήρ ἐστιν
ἀνήρ i.e., Polyphemus
τῷ δ' ὕπνῳ dat. of means
παρειμένος masc. nom. sing. perf. pass. part. < παρίημι

594 παρευτρέπισται 3rd sing. perf. mid./pass. indic. < παρευτρεπίζω
κοὐδὲν ἄλλο = καὶ οὐδὲν ἄλλο; lit., "and (there is) nothing else (to do)"

ἄγε (impera. as adv.), come on!
ἀδάμας, -αντος, ὁ, adamant, steel
ἀναιδής, -ές, shameless
ἄναξ, ἄνακτος, ὁ, lord
ἀπάλαμνος, -ον, irreparable
ἀπαλλάσσω/ἀπαλλάττω, set free of (+ gen.)
ἅπαξ, (adv.), once and for all
αὔλιον, τό, cave, cavern
γείτων, -ονος, ὁ/ἡ, neighbor
δαλός, ὁ, fire-brand, piece of blazing wood
ἐκπαίδευμα, -ατος, τό, child, offspring, nursling
ἐνθάδε (adv.), here
ἔσωθεν (adv./prep. + gen.), within
εὐγενής, -ές, noble
εὐτρεπής, -ές, ready
ἔχω, ἕξω, have
κακός, -ή, -όν, wicked, evil
καπνός, ὁ, smoke
κρέας, τό, (pl. κρέα), meat, piece of meat
λαμπρός, -ά, -όν, bright
λῆμα, τό, will, spirit, courage

μέλας, μέλαινα, μέλαν, dark, black
νύξ, νυκτός, ἡ, night
οἶκος, ὁ, house
ὄμμα, -ατος, τό, eye
ὅπως (+ fut. = urgent exhortation), (see to it) that...
ὄψις, -εως, ἡ, face; vision, eyesight, eye
παρευτρεπίζω, make ready, arrange
παρίημι, relax; (pass.) be relaxed, weakened or exhausted
πάσχω, ἔπαθον, suffer
πατήρ, πατρός, ὁ, father
πλήν (adv.), except, but
πνέω, blow for send forth
πρίν (adv. + inf.), before
πυρόω, burn (w/ fire), set on fire
τέκνον, τό, son, child
ὕπνος, ὁ, sleep
φάρυγξ, φάρυγ(γ)ος, ὁ, throat, gullet
χωρέω, go
ὠθέω, push

---

595 ἔσῃ 2nd sing. fut. mid. (dep.) < εἰμί
596 πέτρας...κἀδάμαντος gens. of material, i.e., "made of..."
κἀδάμαντος = καὶ ἀδάμαντος
597 χώρει note accent
τἀνθάδ' = τὰ ἐνθάδε
599-607 Odysseus prays for success to Hephaestus, "god of fire, whose forge was said to be located under Mt. Aetna and who was thus Polyphemus' neighbor (γείτονος)" (Olson, 68), and Sleep, child of black Night, into whose darkness Odysseus hopes to plunge the Cyclops forever
600 ἀπαλλάχθηθ' 2nd sing. aor. pass. impera. < ἀπαλλάσσω

ἄκρατος ἐλθὲ θηρὶ τῷ θεοστυγεῖ,
καὶ μὴ 'πὶ καλλίστοισι Τρωϊκοῖς πόνοις
αὐτόν τε ναύτας τ' ἀπολέσητ' Ὀδυσσέα
605 ὑπ' ἀνδρὸς ᾧ θεῶν οὐδὲν ἢ βροτῶν μέλει.
ἢ τὴν τύχην μὲν δαίμον' ἡγεῖσθαι χρεών,
τὰ δαιμόνων δὲ τῆς τύχης ἐλάσσονα.

Χορός

λήψεται τὸν τράχηλον
ἐντόνως ὁ καρκίνος
610 τοῦ ξενοδαιτυμόνος· πυρὶ γὰρ τάχα
φωσφόρους ὀλεῖ κόρας.
ἤδη δαλὸς ἠνθρακωμένος
615 κρύπτεται ἐς σποδιάν, δρυὸς ἄσπετον
ἔρνος. ἀλλ' ἴτω Μάρων,
πρασσέτω,

---

602 ἄκρατος the predicate adj. is often used in Gk. where English employs an adv.
θηρὶ τῷ θεοστυγεῖ dat. of disadvantage, i.e., "against..."
604 αὐτόν...Ὀδυσσέα note how Odysseus' talking about himself in the 3rd person and the extreme separation of Odysseus' name from the attributive intensive adj. create a "portentous line [that] is mock-epic in diction and [in] its artificial word order" (O'Sullivan and Collard, 210)
ἀπολέσητ' 2nd pl. aor. act. impera. < ἀπόλλυμι
606 ἢ "or (otherwise)", i.e., "if you should allow me and my men to be destroyed..."
δαίμον' in *apposition* to τύχην
χρεών sc. ἔσται
607 τὰ δαιμόνων lit., "the things of divinities," i.e., "the gods"
τῆς τύχης here, as often in Gk., esp. in verse, the gen. of comparison precedes the comp. adj.

ἄκρατος, -ος, untempered, strong, powerful, violent
ἀνήρ, ἀνδρός, ὁ, man
ἀνθρακόομαι, be burnt to charcoal
ἀπόλλυμι, destroy
ἄσπετος, -ον, unspeakably great or large
βροτός, ὁ, mortal man
δρῦς, δρυός, ἡ, tree
εἶμι, come
ἐλάσσων/ἐλάττων, -ον, (gen. -ονος), inferior to, weaker than (+ gen.)
ἐντόνως (adv.), eagerly, violently
ἐπί (prep. + dat.), after
ἔρνος, -εος, τό, offshoot, shoot
ἔρχομαι, ἦλθον, come
ἤ (conj.), or
ἡγέομαι, believe, regard
ἤδη (adv.), already
θεός, ὁ, god
θεοστυγής, -ές, loathed by the gods, vile
θήρ, θηρός, ἡ, beast, savage

κάλλιστος, -η, -ον, most noble
καρκίνος, ὁ, (pair of) tongs
κόρη, ἡ, pupil
κρύπτω, hide
λαμβάνω, λήψομαι, grasp, seize
μέλω, be an object of care or concern to X (dat.)
ναύτης, -ου, ὁ, sailor
ξενοδαιτυμών, -όνος, ὁ, guest-eater
ὄλλυμι, ὀλῶ, lose
πόνος, ὁ, labor, deed
πῦρ, πυρός, τό, fire
πράσσω, do, act
σποδιά, ἡ, heap of ashes, ash
τράχηλος, ὁ, neck, throat
Τρωϊκός, -ή, -όν, Trojan
τύχη, ἡ, chance
ὑπό (prep. + gen.), at the hands of
φωσφόρος, -ον, light-bringing, shining, bright
χρεών, necessity, fate; + ἐστι, it is necessary, one must (+ inf.)

---

609 καρκίνος either a possible allusion to Hephaestus as blacksmith meting out punishment in the satyrs' imagination (so Olson) or a folk saying expressing the satyrs' hope that Polyphemus "gets it in the neck" (O'Sullivan and Collard)

610 πυρί dat. of means

611 κόρας pl. for sing.; cf. 463 and note ad loc.

613 ἠνθρακωμένος masc. nom. sing. perf. pass. part. < ἀνθρακόομαι

616-8 ἴτω...πρασσέτω...'ξελέτω 3rd sing. act. imperatives < εἶμι, πράσσω, and ἐξαιρέω, respectively (the first two being pres., the last aor.)

616 Μάρων i.e., the wine (given by Maron to Odysseus); an example of *metonomy* (cf. 412)

μαινομένου 'ξελέτω βλέφαρον
Κύκλωπος, ὡς πίῃ κακῶς.
620 κἀγὼ τὸν φιλοκισσοφόρον Βρόμιον
ποθεινὸν εἰσιδεῖν θέλω,
Κύκλωπος λιπὼν ἐρημίαν·
ἆρ' ἐς τοσόνδ' ἀφίξομαι;

Ὀδυσσεύς

σιγᾶτε πρὸς θεῶν, θῆρες, ἡσυχάζετε,
625 συνθέντες ἄρθρα στόματος· οὐδὲ πνεῖν ἐῶ,
οὐ σκαρδαμύσσειν οὐδὲ χρέμπτεσθαί τινα,
ὡς μὴ 'ξεγερθῇ τὸ κακόν, ἔστ' ἂν ὄμματος
ὄψις Κύκλωπος ἐξαμιλληθῇ πυρί.

Χορός

σιγῶμεν ἐγκάψαντες αἰθέρα γνάθοις.

Ὀδυσσεύς

630 ἄγε νυν ὅπως ἅψεσθε τοῦ δαλοῦ χεροῖν
ἔσω μολόντες· διάπυρος δ' ἐστὶν καλῶς.

---

619 ὡς πίῃ κακῶς i.e., so that his drinking costs him in the end
πίῃ aor. subju. in a purp. cl. in primary sequence
620 κἀγώ = καὶ ἐγώ
τὸν φιλοκισσοφόρον "a standard part of Dionysus' iconography" (Olson, 70)
623 τοσόνδ' lit., "so great a thing," i.e., "such happiness/bliss"
συνθέντες masc. nom. pl. aor. act. part. < συντίθημι
625 ἄρθρα στόματος i.e., one's jaws or lips; the phrase seems to be a mock-tragic circumlocution (cf. O'Sullivan and Collard, 213)
626 τινα dir. obj. of ἐῶ
627 'ξεγερθῇ 3rd sing. aor. pass. subju. < ἐξεγείρω

αἰθήρ, -έρος, ἡ, air
ἅπτω, fasten; (mid.) lay hold of, grasp (+ gen.)
ἆρα, (article introducing a question, sometimes adding a skeptical tone)
ἄρθρον, τό, joint
ἀφικνέομαι, ἀφίξομαι, + ἐs/ εἰs, come to, arrive at; attain
βλέφαρον, τό, eyelid, eye
βλώσκω, go
Βρόμιος, ὁ, (common name/epithet of Dionysus) Roarer (< βρόμιος, -α, -ον, noisy, boisterous)
γνάθος, ἡ, jaw
διάπυρος, -ον, red-hot
ἐάω/ἐῶ, allow, permit
ἐγκάπτω, gulp down greedily
εἰσοράω, -εῖδον, look upon, see
εἴσω/ἔσω (adv.), inside
εἶτα (adv.), then
ἐξαιρέω, take out, remove
ἐξαμιλλάομαι, drive out of; (pass.) be rooted out (of/from + gen.)
ἐξεγείρω, wake up X (acc.)

ἐρημία, ἡ, desolate place
ἔστε (conj., w/ ἄν + subju.), until
ἡσυχάζω, be still, keep quiet
θέλω, wish, want (+ inf.)
κακόν, τό, trouble, disaster; monster
κακῶς (adv.), badly
καλῶς (adv.), nicely
λείπω, ἔλιπον, leave (behind)
μαίνομαι, be mad, rage
νυν (adv.), then
πίνω, ἔπιον (aor.), drink
πνέω, breathe
ποθεινός, -ή, -όν, longed for, much desired
πρός (prep. + gen.), by
σιγάω, keep silence, be quiet
σκαρδαμύσσω, blink
στόμα, στόματος, τό, mouth
συντίθημι, put together, close
τοσόσδε, -ήδε, -όνδε, so great
φιλοκισσοφόρος, -ον, fond of wearing ivy
χείρ, χειρός, ἡ, hand
χρέμπτομαι, clear one's throat,
ὡς (conj.), in order that, so that (+ subju. in primary sequence)

---

628 ἐξαμιλληθῇ 3rd sing. aor. pass. subju. < ἐξαμιλλάομαι
629 ἐγκάψαντες αἰθέρα γνάθοις i.e., comic phraseology for holding their breath
  γνάθοις dat. of means
630 χεροῖν dual dat.; dat. of means
631 μολόντες masc. nom. pl. aor. act. part. < βλώσκω

Χορός

οὔκουν σὺ τάξεις οὕστινας πρώτους χρεὼν
καυτὸν μοχλὸν λαβόντας ἐκκάειν τὸ φῶς
Κύκλωπος, ὡς ἂν τῆς τύχης κοινώμεθα;

Χορός α

635   ἡμεῖς μέν ἐσμεν μακροτέρω πρὸ τῶν θυρῶν
ἑστῶτες ὠθεῖν ἐς τὸν ὀφθαλμὸν τὸ πῦρ.

Χορός β

ἡμεῖς δὲ χωλοί γ' ἀρτίως γεγενήμεθα.

Χορός α

ταὐτὸν πεπόνθατ' ἆρ' ἐμοί· τοὺς γὰρ πόδας
ἑστῶτες ἐσπάσθημεν οὐκ οἶδ' ἐξ ὅτου.

Ὀδυσσεύς

640   ἑστῶτες ἐσπάσθητε;

Χορός α

καὶ τά γ' ὄμματα
μέστ' ἐστὶν ἡμῖν κόνεος ἢ τέφρας ποθέν.

Ὀδυσσεύς

ἄνδρες πονηροὶ κοὐδὲν οἵδε σύμμαχοι.

Χορός

ὁτιὴ τὸ νῶτον τὴν ῥάχιν τ' οἰκτίρομεν
καὶ τοὺς ὀδόντας ἐκβαλεῖν οὐ βούλομαι
645   τυπτόμενος, αὕτη γίγνεται πονηρία;

---

634 κοινώμεθα 1st pl. pres. mid./pass. subju. < κοινόω; subju. in purp. cl. (w/ rare inclusion of modal particle ἄν)

635-9 The chorus split into two groups, offering various "lame" excuses for why they should not have to enter the cave and assist Odysseus in blinding the Cyclops

ἀρτίως (adv.), just now
βούλομαι, wish, want
γίγνομαι, be, come to
ἐκβάλλω, ἐξέβαλον, cast out
ἐκκαίω, burn out
θύρα, ἡ, door
ἵστημι, make to stand; (perf. act. w/ pres. sense) stand
καυτός, -ή, -όν, red-hot, burnt
κοινόω, make common; (mid.) take part or share in X (gen.)
κόνις, -εος, ἡ, dust
μακροτέρω (adv.), too far
μεστός, -ή, -όν, full of (+ gen.)
μοχλός, ὁ, stake
νῶτον, τό, back
ὀδούς, -όντος, ὁ, tooth
οἰκτ(ε)ίρω, feel pity for
ὀτιή (conj.; colloquial form of ὅτι), because
οὔκουν (adv.), not therefore? not then?

οὗτος, αὕτη, τοῦτο, this
ὀφθαλμός, ὁ, eye
πάσχω, suffer
ποθεν (adv.), from some place or other
πονηρία, ἡ, cowardice
πονηρός, -ά, -όν, worthless, useless, cowardly
πρό (prep. + gen.), before
πρῶτος, -η, -ον, first
ῥάχις, -εως, ἡ, sprine
σπάω, wrench, dislocate
τάσσω, station, post, or order X (acc.) (to do something + inf.)
τέφρα, ἡ, ash
τύπτω, beat, strike
τύχη, ἡ, good fortune, success
φῶς, φωτός, τό, light
χωλός, -ή, -όν, lame
ὠθέω, push

---

636 ἑστῶτες masc. nom. pl. perf. act. part. < ἵστημι
637 γεγενήμεθα 1st pl. perf. mid. (dep.) indic. < γίγνομαι
638 ταὐτὸν = τὸ αὐτὸ(ν); w/ article (i.e., in the attributive position), αὐτός, αὐτή, αὐτό = "the same (as)" (+ dat.)
πεπόνθατ' 2nd pl. perf. act. indic. < πάσχω
τοὺς...πόδας acc. of respect w/ ἐσπάσθημεν; i.e., we sprained our feet
639 ἐσπάσθημεν 1st pl. aor. pass. indic. < σπάω
ἐξ ὅτου lit., "from what thing," i.e., "from what cause," "why"
641 ἡμῖν dat. of interest (or disadvantage) expressing possession
642 κοὐδέν = καὶ οὐδέν; neut. acc. adj. οὐδέν (an acc. of respect) when used of persons = "good for nothing"
οἴδε σύμμαχοι sc. εἰσι
644 τοὺς ὀδόντας ἐκβαλεῖν i.e., to have my teeth knocked out

ἀλλ' οἶδ' ἐπῳδὴν Ὀρφέως ἀγαθὴν πάνυ,
ὥστ' αὐτόματον τὸν δαλὸν ἐς τὸ κρανίον
στείχονθ' ὑφάπτειν τὸν μονῶπα παῖδα γῆς.

Ὀδυσσεύς

πάλαι μὲν ἤδη σ' ὄντα τοιοῦτον φύσει,
650 νῦν δ' οἶδ' ἄμεινον. τοῖσι δ' οἰκείοις φίλοις
χρῆσθαί μ' ἀνάγκη. χειρὶ δ' εἰ μηδὲν σθένεις,
ἀλλ' οὖν ἐπεγκέλευέ γ', ὡς εὐψυχίαν
φίλων κελευσμοῖς τοῖσι σοῖς κτησώμεθα.

Χορός

δράσω τάδ'. ἐν τῷ Καρὶ κινδυνεύσομεν.
655 κελευσμάτων δ' ἕκατι τυφέσθω Κύκλωψ.

---

646 Ὀρφέως Orpheus' music was said to have had the power to move inanimate objects such as trees and rocks
648 παῖδα γῆς a lineage that can be traced back to Hesiod, *Theogony* 129. O'Sullivan and Collard (216) point out that the many and various "sons of the earth" in Greek mythology are invariably monstrous creatures
ᾔδη 1st sing. pluperf. (w/ imperf. sense) act. < οἶδα
650 ἄμεινον i.e., even better than before
τοῖσι δ' οἰκείοις φίλοις i.e., his crew
651 ἀνάγκη sc. ἐστι
652 γ' "at least"
653 φίλων κελευσμοῖς τοῖσι σοῖς "by means of the exhortations of you, (our) friends"
κτησώμεθα 1st pl. aor. mid. (dep.) subju. < κτάομαι
654 ἐν τῷ Καρὶ κινδυνεύσομεν the idiom ἐν τῷ Καρὶ κινδυνεύειν = "to run the risk (not with one's own person, but) w/ (lit. in) a Carian," i.e., "vicariously," originated from the fact that the people of Caria (a region in western Asia Minor w/ a population of Ionian Greeks, Dorian Greeks, and non-Greek Carians) often hired themselves out

ἀγαθός, -ή, -όν, good, capable
ἄμεινον (adv.), better
ἀνάγκη, ἡ, necessity; w/ ἐστί, it is necessary for X (dat.) to do Y (inf.)
αὐτόματος, -η, -ον, of or by itself
γῆ, ἡ, earth, Earth
δαλός, ὁ, fire-brand, piece of blazing wood
δράω, do
ἕκατι (adv. + preceding gen.), as far as, by means of, by virtue of
ἐπεγκελεύω, encourage, cheer on w/ encouragment
ἐπῳδή, ἡ, incantation, spell
εὐψυχία, ἡ, good courage, high spirits
Κάρ, Καρός, ὁ, Carian
κέλευ(σ)μα, -ατος, τό, exhortation
κελευσμός, ὁ, exhortation, encouragement
κινδυνεύω, run the risk
κρανίον, τό, skull
κτάομαι, get
μηδέν (adv.), not at all
μονώψ, ῶπος, one-eyed
οἰκεῖος, -α, -ον, one's own
Ὀρφεύς, -έως, ὁ, Orpheus
παῖς, παιδός, ὁ, son, child
πάλαι (adv.), for a long time
πάνυ (adv.), very, exceedingly
σθένω, be strong in, have strength in (+ dat.)
στείχω, walk, march, go
τοιοῦτος, -αύτη, -οῦτο(ν), such as this
τύφω, turn into smoke, burn up, burn slowly
ὑφάπτω, stealthily set on fire
φίλος, ὁ, friend
φύσις, φύσεως, ἡ, nature; φύσει, by nature
χράομαι, use (+ dat.)
ὥστε (conj.), (+ inf. = a potential result) so that

---

as mercenaries, and thus were used by other city-states to spare the lives of their own citizen-soldiers

655 κελευσμάτων δ' ἕκατι i.e., "If encouragments can do it" (Kovacs)

τυφέσθω 3rd sing. mid. (= pass.) pres. impera. < τύφω

Χορός
ἰὼ ἰώ·
ὠθεῖτε γενναιότατα,
σπεύδετ᾽, ἐκκαίετ᾽ ὀφρὺν
θηρὸς τοῦ ξενοδαίτα.
τυφέτ᾽ ὦ, καιέτ᾽ ὦ
660   τὸν Αἴτνας μηλονόμον.
τόρνευ᾽ ἕλκε, μὴ ᾽ξοδυνη-
θεὶς δράσῃ τι μάταιον.
Κύκλωψ
ὤμοι, κατηνθρακώμεθ᾽ ὀφθαλμοῦ σέλας.
Χορός
καλός γ᾽ ὁ παιάν· μέλπε μοι τόνδ᾽ αὖ, Κύκλωψ.
Κύκλωψ
665   ὤμοι μάλ᾽, ὡς ὑβρίσμεθ᾽, ὡς ὀλώλαμεν.
ἀλλ᾽ οὔτι μὴ φύγητε τῆσδ᾽ ἔξω πέτρας
χαίροντες, οὐδὲν ὄντες· ἐν πύλαισι γὰρ
σταθεὶς φάραγγος τῆσδ᾽ ἐναρμόσω χέρας.
Χορός
τί χρῆμ᾽ ἀϋτεῖς, ὦ Κύκλωψ;

---

658   ξενοδαίτα = (Doric form of) ξενοδαίτου
660   Αἴτνας = (Doric form of) Αἴτνης
661-2 μὴ...δράσῃ neg. purp. cl., i.e., "lest...," "so that he...not..."
662   ᾽ξοδυνηθεὶς masc. nom. sing. aor. pass. part. < ἐξοδυνάω
663   κατηνθρακώμεθ᾽ an example of *pluralis maiestatis* (so too ὑβρίσμεθ᾽ and ὀλώλαμεν in 665)
        ὀφθαλμοῦ σέλας acc. of respect
664   καλός γ᾽ ὁ παιάν sc. ἐστι
        ὁ παιάν i.e., the Cyclops' screams

Αἴτνη, ἡ, Aetna
αὖ (adv.), again
αὐτέω, cry, shout
γενναιότατα (adv.), most violently
ἕλκω, tear, pull
ἐναρμόζω, fasten
ἐξοδυνάω, ἡ, cause great pain; (pass.) feel great pain, suffer greatly
ἔξω (adv./prep. + gen.), out of
θήρ, θηρός, ἡ, beast, savage
ἵστημι, make to stand; (pass.) stand
ἰώ (exclamation of joy), oh!
κατανθρακόομαι, be burnt to cinders
μάλα (adv.), very much, exceedingly
μάταιος, -α, -ον, rash, outrageous, desperate, reckless
μέλπω, sing
μηλονόμος, -ον, tending goats or sheep
ξενοδαίτης, -ου, ὁ, guest-eater

ὄλλυμι, destroy; (perf. act. w/ mid. sense) perish, be destroyed
οὔτι (adv.), in no way; (+ μή [+ subju.] = emphatic denial) there is no way that...
ὀφρύς, -ύος, ἡ, eyebrow
παιάν, -ᾶνος, ὁ, victory song
πύλη, ἡ, one wing of a pair of double gates; (mostly in pl.) house door, entrance
σέλας, -αος, τό, light, brightness
σπεύδω, hurry
τορνεύω, turn or twist around
ὑβρίζω, treat outrageously, assault violently
φάραγξ, -αγγος, ἡ, cleft, cave
φεύγω, ἔφυγον, flee
χαίρω, rejoice, be glad; (often after a neg. =) unpunished
χρῆμα, -ατος, τό, thing, matter, event; τί χρῆμα, why?
ὦ (exclamation), O!, hey!
ὤμοι (exclamation of surprise, joy, or pain)
ὡς (exclamation), how!

---

665 ὑβρίσμεθ' 1st pl. perf. pass. indic. < ὑβρίζω
     ὀλώλαμεν 1st pl. perf. act. indic. < ὄλλυμι
666-8 Addressed to Odysseus and his crew inside the cave
667 οὐδὲν ὄντες cf. *Od.* 9.515 (Cyclops speaking of Odysseus after his blinding): ἐὼν ὀλίγος τε καὶ οὐτιδανὸς καὶ ἄκικυς ("being small and worthless and weak...")
     ὄντες causal use of the part., i.e., "since you are..."
668 σταθείς masc. nom. sing. aor. pass. part. < ἵστημι
     ἐναρμόσω χέρας sc. to the sides of the cave
     χέρας = (poetic form of) χεῖρας

Κύκλωψ
    ἀπωλόμην.

Χορός
670 αἰσχρός γε φαίνῃ.

Κύκλωψ
    κἀπὶ τοῖσδέ γ' ἄθλιος.

Χορός
μεθύων κατέπεσες ἐς μέσους τοὺς ἄνθρακας;

Κύκλωψ
Οὖτίς μ' ἀπώλεσ'.

Χορός
    οὐκ ἄρ' οὐδείς ⟨σ'⟩ ἠδίκει.

Κύκλωψ
Οὖτίς με τυφλοῖ βλέφαρον.

Χορός
    οὐκ ἄρ' εἶ τυφλός.

Κύκλωψ
†ὡς δὴ σύ†.

Χορός
   καὶ πῶς σ' οὔτις ἂν θείη τυφλόν;

Κύκλωψ
675 σκώπτεις. ὁ δ' Οὖτις ποῦ 'στιν;

Χορός
    οὐδαμοῦ, Κύκλωψ.

---

669 ἀπωλόμην 1st sing. aor. mid. indic. < ἀπόλλυμι
670 κἀπὶ τοῖσδέ γ' ἄθλιος = καὶ ἐπὶ τοῖσδέ γ' ἄθλιος (εἰμί)
672-7 A comically inflected adaptation of *Od.* 9.407-11

ἀδικέω, do X (acc.) wrong, do wrong to X (acc.), wrong, injure
αἰσχρός, -ά, -όν, ugly, awful, terrible
ἄνθραξ, -ακος, ὁ, charcoal, coal
ἀπόλλυμι, ἀπώλεσα, destroy utterly; (mid.) be undone, be ruined
ἄρα (particle), in that case
βλέφαρον, τό, eyelid, eye
ἐπί (prep. + dat.), in addition to
καταπίπτω, κατέπεσον, fall down
μεθύω, be drunk
μέσος, -η, -ον, middle of
οὐδαμοῦ (adv.), nowhere
οὖτις, οὖτι, no one, nobody, nothing
ποῦ (adv.), where?
σκώπτω, mock
τίθημι, make
τυφλός, -ή, -όν, blind
τυφλόω, blind
φαίνω, bring to light; (pass.) be seen (to be), look

672 Οὖτίς see 549 and note ad loc.
οὐκ ἄρ' οὐδείς unlike in English, a compound neg. following another neg. in Gk. does not cancel but instead confirms it
673 τυφλοῖ vivid emphatic pres. (best translated in English as a perf.) w/ (unusually) two dir. objs. (με, βλέφαρον)
674 †ὡς δὴ σύ† lit., "as you in fact!"; "corrupt, but the text clearly conceals an angry response to the satyrs' insistence that Polyphemus cannot be blind." (Olson, 73)
θείη 3rd sing. aor. act. opt. < τίθημι; potential opt.
675 'στιν = ἐστιν

Κύκλωψ
 ὁ ξένος, ἵν' ὀρθῶς ἐκμάθῃς, μ' ἀπώλεσεν,
 ὁ μιαρός, ὅς μοι δοὺς τὸ πῶμα κατέκλυσεν.
Χορός
 δεινὸς γὰρ οἶνος καὶ παλαίεσθαι βαρύς.
Κύκλωψ
 πρὸς θεῶν, πεφεύγασ' ἢ μένουσ' ἔσω δόμων;
Χορός
680 οὗτοι σιωπῇ τὴν πέτραν ἐπήλυγα
 λαβόντες ἑστήκασι.
Κύκλωψ
        ποτέρας τῆς χερός;
Χορός
 ἐν δεξιᾷ σου.
Κύκλωψ
        ποῦ;
Χορός
        πρὸς αὐτῇ τῇ πέτρᾳ.
 ἔχεις;
Κύκλωψ
        κακόν γε πρὸς κακῷ· τὸ κρανίον
 παίσας κατέαγα.
Χορός
        καί σε διαφεύγουσί γε.

---

677 δοὺς masc. nom. sing. aor. act. part. < δίδωμι
678 δεινὸς γὰρ οἶνος sc. ἐστι
    παλαίεσθαι βαρύς sc. ἐστι

αὐτός, -ή, -ό, (intensive adj.) -self; (pl.) –selves; the very one
βαρύς, -εῖα, -ύ, heavy to bear, unbearable, annoying; unpleasant
δεξιά, ἡ, right hand; ἐν δεξιᾷ, on the right
δεινός, -ή, -όν, dangerous, terrible; powerful; marvelous; clever, terribly cunning
διαφεύγω, get away from, escape
δίδωμι, give
δόμος, ὁ, house
εἴσω/ἔσω (adv.; prep. + gen.), within, inside
ἐκμανθάνω, ἐξέμαθον, learn thoroughly, know full well
ἐπῆλυξ, -υγος, sheltering
ἵνα (conj.), so that, in order that (+ subju. in primary sequence)

ἵστημι, make to stand; (perf. act.) stand
κακόν, τό, trouble, disaster
κατάγνυμι, crack in pieces, break; (perf. act.) be broken
κατακλύζω, inundate, drown
λαμβάνω, ἔλαβον, take
μένω, stay, remain
μιαρός, -ή, -όν, defiled w/ blood, polluted; (as a colloquial form of abuse) ὁ μιαρός, the bastard
ὀρθῶς (adv.), really, truly
παίω, strike, hit
παλαίω, wrestle; (pass.) to be beaten (at wrestling)
πότερος, -α, -ον, which of the two
πρός (prep. + gen.), by; (+ dat.) at, near; on top of, in addition to
πῶμα, -ατος, τό, drink
σιωπῇ (adv.), in silence

---

679 πεφεύγασ' 3rd pl. perf. act. indic. < φεύγω
     δόμων poet. pl. for sing.
680 οὗτοι often much like an adv., in local sense, i.e., "here"
     ἐπήλυγα predicative adj. of τὴν πέτραν, i.e., "as a shelter"
681 ἑστήκασι 3rd pl. perf. act. indic. < ἵστημι
     ποτέρας τῆς χερός; i.e., to my left or right?
683 ἔχεις; sc. them
     κακόν γε πρὸς κακῷ sc. ἔχω
684 κατέαγα 1st sing. perf. act. indic. < κατάγνυμι

Κύκλωψ
685   οὐ τῇδέ πῃ, τῇδ' εἶπας;
Χορός
                    οὔ· ταύτῃ λέγω.
Κύκλωψ
    πῇ γάρ;
Χορός
            περιάγου κεῖσε, πρὸς τἀριστερά.
Κύκλωψ
    οἴμοι γελῶμαι· κερτομεῖτέ μ' ἐν κακοῖς.
Χορός
    ἀλλ' οὐκέτ', ἀλλὰ πρόσθεν οὗτός ἐστι σοῦ.
Κύκλωψ
    ὦ παγκάκιστε, ποῦ ποτ' εἶ;
Ὀδυσσεύς
                        τηλοῦ σέθεν
690 φυλακαῖσι φρουρῶ σῶμ' Ὀδυσσέως τόδε.
Κύκλωψ
    πῶς εἶπας; ὄνομα μεταβαλὼν καινὸν λέγεις.
Ὀδυσσεύς
    ὅπερ μ' ὁ φύσας ὠνόμαζ' Ὀδυσσέα,
    δώσειν δ' ἔμελλες ἀνοσίου δαιτὸς δίκας·
    κακῶς γὰρ ἂν Τροίαν γε διεπυρώσαμεν
695 εἰ μή σ' ἑταίρων φόνον ἐτιμωρησάμην.

---

685   τῇδέ πῃ, τῇδ' εἶπας note *alliteration*
686   γάρ "then"
       περιάγου 2nd sing. pres. mid. impera. < περιάγω

ἀνόσιος, -ον, unholy, impious
ἀριστερά, τά, left
γελάω, laugh (at), deride
δαίς, δαιτός, ἡ, banquet, feast
διαπυρόω, destroy by fire
δίδωμι, give; + δίκας, pay the penalty, suffer punishment
δίκη, ἡ, penalty (for + gen.)
ἑταῖρος, ὁ, comrade, companion
καινός, -ή, -όν, new
κακῶς (adv.), uselessly, to no purpose
κεῖσε (adv.), this way
κερτομέω/κερτομῶ, taunt
μέλλω, be destined or bound (+ inf., usu. fut.)
μεταβάλλω, μετέβαλον, alter, change
οἴμοι (exclamation of pain, fright, pity, anger, grief, or surprise)
ὄνομα, -ατος, τό, name
ὀνομάζω, name, call
ὅσπερ, ἥπερ, ὅπερ, the very one who, the very one/thing which

οὐκέτι (adv.), no longer
παγκάκιστος, -ον, utterly bad, most evil or wicked
περιάγω, turn around
πη (particle), somewhere
πῇ (particle), where? in which way?
ποτέ (particle), ever
πρόσθεν (adv./prep. + gen.), before, in front of
σῶμα, -ατος, τό, body
ταύτῃ (adv.), here, in this direction
τῇδε (adv.), here, in this direction
τηλοῦ (adv./prep. + gen.), far from
τιμωρέω, avenge; (mid.) take vengeance on someone (acc.) for something (acc.)
φόνος, murder
φρουρέω/φρουρῶ, watch, guard
φυλακή, ἡ, guarding
φύω, beget, engender; ὁ φύσας, the father

---

686 τἀριστερά = τὰ ἀριστερά
688 οὐκέτ' sc. κερτομῶ σε
οὗτός often much like an adv., in local sense, i.e., "here"
689 σέθεν = σοῦ
690 φυλακαῖσι φρουρῶ lit., "I guard w/ guardings." The "mild tautology.. [is] perhaps...a form of emphasis." (O'Sullivan and Collard, 223)
693 Note *alliteration, assonance,* and *hyperbaton* (δώσειν... δίκας)
δώσειν fut. act. inf. < δίδωμι
694-5 C-to-F condit.
διεπυρώσαμεν...ἐτιμωρησάμην note end-rhyme, for emphasis

Κύκλωψ
αἰαῖ· παλαιὸς χρησμὸς ἐκπεραίνεται·
τυφλὴν γὰρ ὄψιν ἐκ σέθεν σχήσειν μ' ἔφη
Τροίας ἀφορμηθέντος. ἀλλὰ καὶ σέ τοι
δίκας ὑφέξειν ἀντὶ τῶνδ' ἐθέσπισεν,
700 πολὺν θαλάσσῃ χρόνον ἐναιωρούμενον.
Ὀδυσσεύς
κλαίειν σ' ἄνωγα· καὶ δέδραχ' ὅπερ λέγεις.
ἐγὼ δ' ἐπ' ἀκτὰς εἶμι καὶ νεὼς σκάφος
ἥσω 'πὶ πόντον Σικελὸν ἔς τ' ἐμὴν πάτραν.
Κύκλωψ
οὐ δῆτ', ἐπεί σε τῆσδ' ἀπορρήξας πέτρας
705 αὐτοῖσι συνναύταισι συντρίψω βαλών.
ἄνω δ' ἐπ' ὄχθον εἶμι, καίπερ ὢν τυφλός,
δι' ἀμφιτρῆτος τῆσδε προσβαίνων ποδί.
Χορός
ἡμεῖς δὲ συνναῦταί γε τοῦδ' Ὀδυσσέως
ὄντες τὸ λοιπὸν Βακχίῳ δουλεύσομεν.

696-700 Adapted from *Od.* 9.506-12, 532-5
697 τυφλὴν...ἔφη = γὰρ ἔφη μ' σχήσειν τυφλὴν ὄψιν ἐκ σέθεν
ἐκ σέθεν "by you"
σχήσειν fut. act. inf. < ἔχω
700 Note interlocked word order
πολὺν...χρόνον acc. of duration of time
701 κλαίειν ἄνωγα i.e., "I tell you to go to hell!"; for the colloquialism, see 174 and note ad loc.
δέδραχ' 1st sing. perf. act. indic. < δράω
ὅπερ λέγεις i.e., Polyphemus' words at 697-8
704-7 Adapted from *Od.* 9.481-3, 537-40

αἰαῖ (exclamation of horror or surprise), ah!
ἀκτή, ἡ, headland, promontory; (pl.) the coast
ἀμφιτρής, -ῆτος, pierced from end to end, w/ a double entrance
ἀντί (prep. + gen.), for, for the sake of
ἄνω (adv.), up
ἄνωγα (perf. w/ pres. sense), command, order, urge
ἀπορρήγνυμι, ἀπέρρηξα, break off (a piece) from (+ gen.)
ἀφορμάω, make to start from; (pass.) depart from (+ gen.)
βάλλω, strike
δῆτα (particle), truly, certainly; (w/ neg.) certainly not, no indeed
δουλεύω, serve (+ dat.), be a slave to (+ dat.)
εἶμι, will go
ἐκπεραίνω, finish off; (pass.) be fulfilled
ἐναιωρέομαι, float or drift about in (+ dat.)
ἐπεί (conj.), since
ἔχω, have
θάλασσα, ἡ, sea

θεσπίζω, prophesy, foretell
ἵημι, ἥσω, send
καίπερ (particle, usu. w/ part.), although
κλαίω, cry, wail
λοιπόν (adv., w/ or w/out article τό), in the future, for the future
ὄχθος, ὁ, hill
ὄψις, -εως, ἡ, vision, eyesight, eye
παλαιός, -ά, -όν, ancient
πάτρα, ἡ, fatherland, native land
πόντος, ὁ, sea
πούς, ποδός, ὁ, foot
προσβαίνω, approach, ascend, climb
Σικελός, -ή, -όν, of Sicily, Sicilian
σκάφος, -εος, τό, hull (of a ship)
συνναύτης, ου, ὁ, shipmate
συντρίβω, crush X (acc.) together w/ Y (dat.)
τοι (particle), then, in fact
ὑπέχω, furnish, supply; + δίκας, pay or incur a penalty
χρησμός, ὁ, oracle, prophecy
χρόνος, ὁ, time

---

707 ἀμφιτρῆτος τῆσδε sc. πέτρας; i.e., the Cyclop's cave, which, rather peculiarly at this point, is said to have two entrances (cf. 666-8)

ποδί dat. of means (somewhat pleonastic w/ προσβαίνων)

709 δουλεύσομεν "The play ends on a note of mild ring composition and paradox, whereby slavery, emphasized in the satyrs' description of their plight at the outset (23-6), 78-81, cf. 442, etc.), resurfaces at the very moment of their escape. But this 'slavery' means a return to the joys of life under their natural master, Dionysus (cf. 429-30), and liberation from the brutal despotism of the Cyclops." (O'Sullivan and Collard, 226)

OTHER ANCIENT GREEK AND LATIN INTERMEDIATE READERS BY THE AUTHOR

ANCIENT GREEK

The Infancy Gospel of Thomas

The Infancy Gospel of Thomas (c. 150 CE) is an excellent text for students who have completed the first year of college-level Ancient Greek. Its length is short, its syntax is generally straightforward, and its narrative is inherently interesting, for it is the only account from the period of early Christianity that tells of the childhood of Jesus. This student edition includes grammatical, syntactical, literary, historical, and cultural notes. Complete vocabulary is provided for each section of the text, with special attention paid to the differences between Koine Greek and Classical Greek meanings and usage. Since *The Infancy Gospel of Thomas* possesses an unusually rich textual history, this edition also includes a selection of the most interesting variant readings.

Lucian, *On the Death of Peregrinus*

Lucian's *On the Death of Peregrinus* is an excellent text for students who have completed the first year of college-level Ancient Greek or its equivalent. Its length is relatively short, its syntax is generally straightforward, and its narrative is inherently interesting, for it recounts the life of a man who was so determined to establish a new religious cult to himself that he committed suicide at the Olympic Games in 165 CE by self-immolation. Lucian, an eyewitness to this event, depicts Peregrinus as a glory-obsessed impostor who began his career as an adulterer, pederast, and parricide before becoming a leader of the Christian Church, a Cynic philosopher, and an aspiring "divine guardian of the night." Also of interest to readers today is that Lucian's text contains some of the earliest and most fascinating comments made by a member of the Greco-Roman educated elite concerning Jesus and the Christians of the 2nd century CE. This edition includes grammatical, syntactical, literary, historical, and cultural notes. Vocabulary lists are provided for each section of the text, with a glossary of all words at the end.

Lucian, *True Stories*

Lucian's *True Stories* is an excellent text for students who have completed the first year of college-level Ancient Greek or its equivalent. Its length is relatively modest, its syntax is generally straightforward, and its narrative – a sophisticated satire that blends elements of fantasy and science fiction – is both engaging and thought-provoking. This edition includes extensive grammatical, syntactical, rhetorical, literary, historical, biographical, and cultural notes. Complete vocabulary is provided for each section of the text, with special attention paid to Lucian's comic verbal coinages. Since Lucian's *True Stories* abounds with references to and appropriations from nine centuries of Ancient Greek literature, this edition also includes a generous selection of comparative passages (including the entirety of Iambulus' "Journey to the Islands of the Sun") to assist the student in appreciating still more this cunningly crafted and densely allusive work.

Xenophon of Ephesus, *An Ephesian Tale*

Xenophon of Ephesus's "pulp-fiction" novel, *An Ephesian Tale*, is an excellent text for students who have completed the first year of college-level Ancient Greek or its equivalent. Its length is quite short, its syntax is straightforward, and its narrative – an adventure romance between two young ill-starred lovers (Habrocomes and Anthia) – is one of the most action-packed and enjoyable in all of Ancient Greek literature. This edition includes brief grammatical, syntactical, rhetorical, and cultural notes. Complete vocabulary is provided for each section of the text.

Aesop's Fables (a selection)

This book, containing 35 Aesopic fables/versions of fables, is designed for students who, at a minimum, are finishing, or who have just finished, the first year (or the high school equivalent) of college Ancient Greek. It is also for individuals who studied Ancient Greek years ago and would like to return to the language and its literature in as easy and engaging a manner as possible. In order to serve better the needs of such readers as these, numerous grammatical and syntactical notes, along with extensive vocabulary lists, have been provided.

A special feature of this text is the generous selection of different versions of the fables that have been created over time. Although many of these are retellings of the same fable in Ancient Greek (some of which are in verse), six come from La Fontaine's celebrated French versions as recently translated with great verve by Craig Hill. The vast majority of these different versions, however, are from the rich tradition of English translations/adaptations made between the 17th and 20th centuries.

Another special feature if the inclusion of a substantial number of illustrations from the 18th to the 20th centuries that showcase the various approaches artists have employed in illuminating the fables.

Ancient Greek Cyclops Tales

This collection of Ancient Greek "Cyclopea," the companion volume to *Euripides: Cyclops*, contains the following works: Homer, *Odyssey* 9.105-566; Theocritus, *Idylls* 6 and 11; Callimachus, Epigram 46 Pf./G-P 3; Lucian, *Dialogues of the Sea-Gods* 1 and 2). In addition to providing an introduction to each of these texts, the commentaries include extensive grammatical, lexical, and metrical assistance, with notes focusing on the thematic and intertextual connections between these various works.

Ancient Greek Lyric Poetry (a selection)

[forthcoming]

Cebes' Tablet

[forthcoming]

LATIN

A Medieval Latin Miscellany (with Art Robson)

This Medieval Latin reader is aimed at intermediate undergraduate/advanced high school Latin students. The texts included in this collection cover religious biography (excerpts from Jerome's *Life of Hilarion*), tall-tales (*Asinarius* and *Rapularius*), heroic journey (*Alexander the Great Meets Thalestris, Queen of the Amazons* and Letaldus of Micy's *The Fisherman Swallowed by a Whale*), fables (Odo of Cheriton) and jokes (Poggio Bracciolini). Introductions to each text, as well as assistance with vocabulary, grammar, and syntax are provided.

Three Medieval Latin Liturgical Dramas

This edition makes available to intermediate Latin students three dramatic works of Medieval Latin literature. The earliest of these, the eleventh-century *Tres Clerici* ("The Three Students"), recounts one of the miracles of that most popular of medieval saints, Nicholas. This drama's economical construction and refined use of a simple metrical unit exemplify how a playwright can convey much in few words. The other two plays included in this collection are the outstanding examples of Latin liturgical drama composed in the twelfth century. The *Danielis Ludus* ("The Play of Daniel"), written in the cathedral school of Beauvais, adapts material from the Bible to relate the meaning of a story from the ancient past – the Hebrew prophet Daniel's interactions with two foreign rulers, Belshazzar and Darius – to contemporary issues. This play's rhetorical sophistication, metrical variety, and musical invention are unsurpassed in the dramatic works from this period. Hildegard of Bingen's *Ordo Virtutum* ("The Play of the Virtues") has the distinction of being the only play in this group whose author is not anonymous. Hildegard left behind more than just a name, however, for her impressive literary, scientific, theological, and musical oeuvre rivals those of her more traditionally educated male peers in quality and surpasses them in diversity. In addition, Hildegard's female-centered play, whose verses are rich with symbolism, fuses together liturgical drama and theological allegory in an innovative manner that anticipates the new genre of morality plays written in the vernacular languages two centuries later. This edition provides significant assistance with vocabulary, grammar, and syntax, with special attention paid to Medieval Latin forms. There are also extensive literary and historical notes.

Gesta Francorum:
An Eyewitness Account of the First Crusade

[forthcoming]

Made in the USA
Las Vegas, NV
07 January 2025